Laura invited me to be on the board of Street Books and I asked how it was done. Did we all go to a graveyard at midnight on Halloween with a dead cat? And she said, "No cat ritual, we just say it's okay and then it is."

"Well good," I said. "Lucky for the cat, I guess."

BEN HODGSON & LAURA MOULTON

LOANERS

The Making of a Street Library

a Street Books book, in collaboration with Perfect Day Publishing
© Ben Hodgson & Laura Moulton 2021
The moral rights of the authors have been asserted.

Portions of this book first appeared in different form in *Street Roots*, *Oregon Humanities*, and in an interview with *Hinchas de Poesía*. This book was partially funded by a grant from the Regional Arts & Culture Council. Several names and identifying characteristics have been changed, and the chronology has occasionally been compressed for clarity.

Loaners: the Making of a Street Library / Ben Hodgson & Laura Moulton
ISBN: 978-0-9836327-9-5
Library of Congress Control Number: 2021939073

First printing October 2021

Cover design and illustrations by Aaron Robert Miller
Photo by Eli Haan
Copyedited by Esa Grigsby
Edited by Alissa Hattman & Michael Heald

Printed by Worzalla in the United States of America

www.streetbooks.org
www.lauramoulton.org
www.perfectdaypublishing.com

for my family
—Laura

to Bonnie Hope Hodgson (1942–1958)
—Ben

ONE

THREE-DAY NOTICE (BEN)

Soft landings. That's what I'm all about, but this was not going to be a soft landing. This was going to be the hardest landing I ever landed on. It's a well-known story: A man ends up downtown on skid row, starts hitting the bottle, and never comes back. But this was much worse. When I hit the streets, I *stopped* drinking. Now you know that's a desperate man, who feels so bad that he stops drinking, like a country song in reverse. There wasn't anything to party about, and I didn't need no damn weed to heighten the sensation of how lousy I was feeling. I spent a good deal of time wondering what had gone wrong and how come I didn't see it coming, then realized that I had seen it coming, for nearly twelve weeks. I remembered how I'd gradually dissolved into panic and collapse. Scrambling around trying to find a job, even though in the back of my mind I could feel the time running out faster than I could catch up. Then one day a three-day notice was taped to the door and all I could do was pack up and go.

I was so out of it I couldn't even bring myself to give the key back to the manager and tell them I was leaving. And the things I left behind: Sid's briefcase, Dave's doctor bag, Brian's record collection, and my photo album. Silly sentimental attachments? Of course, in the one sense, and in the other sense, a damn disgrace—those were the last things I had of my brothers.

With a change of clothes and a couple of blankets, I shipped off to the Baltic and Mediterranean of Portland, which is Old Town, just two squares away from the Pearl. I was in it up to my neck. Everything had piled up on me, like I was buried under a huge stinking pile of garbage. I was going to have to try and dig my way out of it, like some mole.

That was about as fine as my finer points got for a good long while, till I got settled in. Finding some place to sleep every night, at first near the Portland Rescue Mission, sticking close to the crowd. Carving out my space every night. Up and down the sidewalk, maybe near the door where the guy that talks to himself stays, or down around the corner, where this girl walks back and forth making chicken noises. If that didn't work, I could take my chances under the bridge and try and sleep while some guy that's five-fourths drunk would commence bellyaching about the world in general.

I'm not kidding about the chicken girl. I was trying to sleep one night while this hopelessly drugged-out woman was pacing around making chicken noises. I finally got up to move, and I told the two guys next to me, "She's going to do this all night." Saw the guys the next morning and they told me they should have moved too, because it was just like I said: The chicken girl had gone on for eight doggone hours with the chicken noises.

Hey, better living through chemistry, right?

THE NUMBERS (Laura)

In 2008, the recession swept through the country and left in its wake more than three million foreclosures. In 2009, Oregon ranked first in the nation per capita for people experiencing houselessness. As time wore on, the number of people living on the street in Portland steadily increased, and by January 2011, the city's one-night count of people outside, in shelters, and cars tallied 4,655.

Back in 2010, after their previous efforts had been ruled unconstitutional, the Portland City Council passed an updated sit-lie ordinance that required people to leave a six- to eight-foot zone of sidewalk open, though it did allow for a person to sit or lie down at the outer edge. The rule was enforced between 7:00 a.m. and 9:00 p.m. and violators received a $250 ticket and community service. Bike rangers glided through parks and public spaces, watching for drug dealing or physical altercations, issuing exclusion orders that would ban a person from a space for up to six months. The Clean & Safe guys, many of them freshly transitioned from the streets themselves, pedaled their own tricycle carts full of cleaning supplies around, pausing here and there to scrub gum off a surface or pick up litter.

At the time, my kids were four and seven years old. My husband and I were raising them in a cozy house with chickens in our yard. Our lives were a kind of happy chaos, and the idea of taking on larger social problems stayed at the periphery. But every night when I tucked my kids into their warm beds, I thought of the people I'd seen downtown.

Scientists estimate the human eye processes an image in something like thirteen milliseconds. I think that's about all the time it takes for people to decide what a blue tarp draped over a shopping cart means for the person standing next to it. Add a cardboard sign, and it completed the snapshot of a tough spot. A metaphor for the margins, a displacement, something dropping into a crack.

FLAT TIRE (BEN)

In 1998, I got hired on as a draftsman at a wafer fab that was being built in Eugene, which was a splendid career move for me at the time.

My first mistake was the same one I always make: I got way ahead of myself. Rather than stay at my friend's place until I was on sound financial footing, I swapped the Lincoln for his old trailer and moved into a trailer park, so as to be in my own place and not impose on his domicile. The move was premature. For one thing, I couldn't even afford the monthly rate at the park, and had to pay the slightly higher weekly rate. I should have simply waited until I could've gotten my own apartment in the first place.

This particular trailer park, I found out too late, was in a state of transition. They'd had so many hassles, police calls and so forth, that they were in the process of trying to change to retirement-age tenants, and were jumping at any excuse to get rid of the younger set. That made my second mistake particularly telling.

All I did was forget to fax my time sheet to the temp service. You mailed it to them to make it official, but you had to fax it first to get your check on time. My check was late, so my week's rent was late, and the trailer park management jumped on the pretext to evict.

The stress of moving, the stress of a new job, me working probably too hard in order to make a good impression, multitudinous stresses piling up, and I was coming unglued. The darn thing is, we were romping and stomping on the job, but the offsite problems became intolerable, and I crumbled.

Moved to another trailer park, then a third one, then they impounded the trailer, then I got fired. Next thing you know, I'm living in my car.

It was springtime in Creswell, busting out all over with blossoms, but still cold at night. I kept warm by starting the engine and running the heater, then turning off the ignition when it was warm enough. I had it parked in the parking lot of the bar, and the town fathers put up with my intrusion. I still don't know how the fire started, maybe the engine overheated, but I woke up to a conflagration. I ran into the bar to call the authorities and returned to watch my car burn up. The fire truck got there and doused the flames. A crowd gathered and I overheard someone say, "What's he gonna do now? He was living in that thing!"

The car was totaled. Everything under the hood was gone, all the wires, even the battery. The tires were gone, it was sitting on the rims. As a firefighter was leaving, I caught his attention and sang out, "Any of you guys bring a can of Fix-a-Flat?"

The guy laughed and said, "I don't think that's going to help much."

THE BIG SKY (LAURA)

The seed of the street library was probably planted before Portland, when I lived in Provo, Utah and worked at the Food & Shelter Coalition. My job was to arrange emergency housing and set up volunteers to serve meals, but I also soaked in the stories of the people who came through. It's where I met Urban Robbin and TJ Reynolds, both in their late seventies. There they were, crafting their days from nothing, with no particular place to go. Urban was squatting in a concrete basement and rode a kid's bicycle with a banana seat. TJ crushed up iced animal cookies in his chili and sang "Down by the Old Mill Stream." I looked forward to their stories each day because they felt like the most authentic characters I knew. My longing for people living real, sometimes roughshod lives, may have had to do with the artificiality of the rest of my day. At the time, I was attending a religious university, where a sea of shiny people with very good attitudes marched to and from their classes on campus. It was the early nineties.

Fast forward to 1999, when I lived with my boyfriend, Ben, and one each of our younger brothers in a house in inner Southeast Portland. I volunteered at the community radio station, KBOO, where I learned how to produce features and mix programs on the boards. I anchored the news every Wednesday night and once, on a broadcast, pronounced the Irish political party Sinn Féin, just like it looks: "Sin Fine," instead of "Shin Feign." It was bad. I repeated it several times and my co-anchor winced each time. But they couldn't fire me because I was a volunteer. On my way to and from the radio station, I'd pass through the courtyard of St. Francis of Assisi Parish and greet the folks who gathered outside with their bedrolls and dogs and shopping carts, tarps, and heavy boots. I decided to see if anyone would be game to have a conversation with me, so I could create a radio feature composed of their stories for KBOO's annual "Homelessness Marathon." That's how I met Quiet Joe. As I stood peering into the dining hall, trying to get my nerve up to approach the guys, he said, "You're welcome to go in if you need a bite to eat."

Joe told me that he'd lived outside by choice for fourteen years, was originally from the East, and preferred to live outdoors and not have to pay someone else for a roof or utilities or that sort of thing. He found scrap metal and wire to recycle, and he made an okay living at this. We talked about books we liked, and discovered that we had a favorite author in common, the western writer A. B. Guthrie Jr. Later, I reflected on our conversation and realized that it was surprise I'd experienced at learning we'd both liked Guthrie's novel *The Big Sky* the best. This bothered me. What had I assumed about Quiet Joe before we'd had a conversation? Some weeks later, I found a few Guthrie titles at a used bookstore, tucked them into a brown paper bag, and passed them to Joe the next time I saw him.

TOWN CLOWN (BEN)

I wasn't quite finished with Creswell yet. Even in a place that small there were a few itinerants, mostly staying off to the side except for Monty, the town clown. He had unofficial permission to stay in the backyard at the house of a woman who had died, and that was where I went after my car got torched. I shuffled around a couple different jobs until I eventually got picked up at the chicken plant. They had gotten tired of the immigration raids and had finally decided to start offering a living wage to their workers, so a lot of the locals started hiring on. It was a visceral sensation wading through all that viscera, but it paid.

The job kept me going for most of a season, and then one day someone came by who had known the boss from somewhere before and needed a job, so they took him on and let me go, and I was back on the train tracks. Portland was beckoning, but as is my custom, I took the long way around to get there. By way of Sacramento and Phoenix and back, and then later by way of Sacramento and Idaho Falls and back. When one of your middle names is Forwarding Address, it only takes twelve years to do all that.

I must have picked that up from Tolstoy or something. If you can't change the world, change yourself. And if you can't change yourself change your address. That's the painless way to break up with your woman. No honey, I haven't changed, it's my address that's changing.

PORTLAND, 1999 (Laura)

Along with our brothers, Ben and I rented a big foursquare on SE Oak Street, with dark wood floors and a front porch with peeling paint. It was across the street from the Anne Hughes Kitchen Table Café, and once in a while we'd drift over there for a coffee or Anne would invite us to one of her roundtable soup nights.

One day, a guy named Michael knocked. I opened the door to find him swaying a bit unsteadily, a bandage on his head and a hospital band on his wrist. Poking out from underneath his sweatshirt and tucked into oversized jeans was a faded hospital gown.

"Have you got any work you need done around here?" he asked.

I looked at the yard, which was mostly packed dirt. "We don't really think about the yard much," I told him. "To be honest, we don't really notice it."

I'd had conversations with Michael before, since he was sleeping outside in the courtyard at St. Francis. He'd mentioned that he sometimes spent time at the Jolly Roger, a bar down the street frequented by Harley Davidson riders. I had a sudden inspiration. At a literary event earlier that month, I'd won two pairs of leather Harley gloves in a raffle. Since our bicycles were our sole means of transportation, it was hard conjuring a scenario in which any of us would wear the gloves.

"Hold on a second," I said. I ran upstairs to get them from my dresser and returned to the porch and held them out. "If you want to see what you can get for these at the Jolly Roger, we can split the proceeds."

Michael took the gloves and examined them, then grinned. "You're on."

A few days later, my brother Mark said, "Hey, you had a visitor today. Said his name was Michael? He just wanted you to know he's still working on selling the gloves, but that he'll definitely bring you some money."

A few days after that, Michael brought me fifteen dollars.

CARDBOARD (BEN)

I saw everybody carrying cardboard around and using it to sleep on, but I didn't see the sense of it. As padding it looked completely ineffective. A few months later, when I finally tried it myself, I saw the sense of it immediately. It's not the padding, it's the temperature. The sidewalk is very cold, and it wants to draw all the heat out of your body. It's that little bit of insulation that makes a tremendous difference, maybe fifteen degrees or more, and, in a flash, cardboard went from a curiosity to a necessity, and the getting of it became a daily ritual. And a chore, and a problem. All that cardboard gets thrown out every morning and you have to find more every evening.

PORTLAND, 2010 (LAURA)

My son, Coen, was a first grader in the Spanish immersion program at the beleaguered little elementary school across the street. They required uniforms, so I was kept busy trying to send him in khaki pants and a navy or white polo shirt. My daughter, Sylvie, went to a Waldorf-inspired preschool twice a week where everybody brought their lunches in little baskets and nobody used plastic wrap. Everything inside the classroom was soft and pastel, no sharp edges. Baskets of horse chestnuts and wooden blocks to play with. My mother-in-law was sponsoring Suzuki violin lessons, so once a week I drove the kids to Southeast and they got a half hour each with their teacher, Annalisa. At home, they each had a sticker chart with a square for every day they practiced.

Three of our six chickens kept getting out of the coop: Franny, Gillian, and Zooey. So we trimmed one wing each, the kids helping me hold them; later on, I discovered the feathers arranged on the couch by one of the kids. I couldn't keep track of domestic life. Days were composed of scattering corn scratch for the chickens outside, letting them out of their coop, breakfast for the kids inside, packing lunches, sending them into the world, greeting them again, carpet-press to blow off stress, playing with Legos, suppertime, bath time, story hour, tuck into bed. Repeat.

I was also working with Literary Arts, teaching a writing residency at Lincoln High School in collaboration with the art museum, which meant we could occupy whichever gallery we wanted for the class—a dream gig. But, since Ben was working full-time, whenever I took on teaching assignments during this era, things started to pile up on the domestic front. So much so that the same day I found a fan of feathers on the couch, I also finally got to the bottom of what stank in the fridge—beans, it turned out—I opened the container and suffered beanlash.

My head was full of the art I saw that day: Mickalene Thomas's rhinestone "Oprah Winfrey" and Kara Walker's steel cut black figures in "Burning African Village Play Set with Big House and Lynching." This was what I was thinking about while pushing a newly purchased stain stick around on a white shirt of Coen's.

Corn scratch, feathers, white shirt stained with paint. It felt as if each scene of my day had occurred in real time and then disgorged some piece of evidence at the end of it, as if to prove it had happened. I felt like an unwilling detective in a mystery I was too tired to solve. But in the midst of the domestic chaos, I still had ideas I wanted to try out, creative schemes that came to me after hours. I didn't want to let go of this impulse, no matter how many other things competed for my attention.

ÉQUIPAGE PATHÉTIQUE (BEN)

I had been outdoors for about nine months by then, and still hadn't recovered from the nasty shock of falling into the bottom of the barrel and then seeping on down through the cracks. I slept in Old Town, with a few spare clothes and a couple of blankets. Most nights, the sidewalks from the bridge and around Second Avenue to Couch were haphazardly strewn with various specimens of humanity, some of whom a chagrined creator might have called failed experiments. I was usually the third or fourth experiment down from the Mission.

To a new guy, just finding a spot was a source of anxiety. I soon enough worked out a simple four-step routine. Breakfast at the Mission, 7:00 a.m. Kill time. Dinner at the Mission, 6:00 p.m. Find a spot on the sidewalk. This was challenging. Wasn't two weeks before I was on Burnside over the MAX tracks, when Andre Payton came to a bad end. Corner of Second and Couch. They counted dozens of bullets. Welcome to Old Town.

There were a few doorways on Third between Couch and Davis, good rain spots, availability various. I commandeered one of them and it turned into "my" spot, even though there is really no such thing as a reserved spot. Think this one over: If you have to go to the bathroom in the middle of the night, you can go to one of the nearby johns, and when you get back, maybe some of your stuff is missing. Or you can take everything with you, and when you get back, maybe someone is in your spot. Or you can just give up and let fly whenever and wherever you have to. What I had taken to doing was not drinking anything past about noon. Not the healthiest approach, but it does show initiative, and employers take that into consideration.

Gotta hand it to the cops, it was fairly slick how they did it. Showed up about 4:00 a.m. and started rousting people, one at a time, handing out exclusions, so you don't even know they're there until it's your turn. You see, under the bridge is considered part of Waterfront Park. Park closes at midnight. So now I couldn't be in the park, any part of it, day or night, for six months. Bummer.

Didn't know where I was going to sleep, so I went back to the sidewalks around the Mission and the overflow under the bridge at the Skidmore MAX stop near the Mission. Under the bridge there were some aggressive types, usually the drinkers, that got belligerent, and it was a creepy place in general. That night there was a confrontation I overheard that sounded like someone had pulled a knife, because I heard a girl say, "Do it. You don't have the balls." Then I heard the sound of someone falling down. I heard these things. But I did not lift my head to see what was happening.

Somebody stole a bike right in front of me the next night. I had heard a couple of guys talking about the bike earlier, when locking it up for the night on one of those hitching posts. The owner was only about twenty feet from me on the sidewalk there on Second. Late that night, I woke to see a couple of people there by the bike, one of them with a pair of bolt cutters, at work on the chain. I heard the chain give way, and a girl's voice say, "Yeah." They walked off with it. You have to be impressed at my courage; I never made a sound.

Seems despicable but stick around: It gets better. Not long after the bike theft, I saw a guy step over the seawall along the Willamette, just north of Burnside, and look around, thinking it over. I walked right on past and on down to my usual bench and opened my book; when I looked back, there was no one there. I didn't even check to see if he had jumped (he had) or if somebody should make a phone call or something (they fished him out). What was I supposed to do? Get involved? I wouldn't have known whether to try and talk him out of it or ask him to save me a seat.

BUILDING THE LIBRARY (LAURA)

I was spread pretty thin already, but I'd begun to experiment with socially engaged art projects, work that ventured out of the traditional spaces of studio or gallery and into the streets. My interest in these sorts of projects dated all the way back to my early days in Portland, when Ben and I had launched his brainchild, Gumball Poetry, a poetry journal published into gumball machines that lived in bookstores and cafés in Portland and other cities. More recently, with the help of my brother James, I'd created a giant rolling mobile gallery for Portland State University. It displayed objects collected from PSU students in tiny plexiglass windows: socks with text that read YOU CAN'T AFFORD ME, a crucifix, a ceramic dinosaur mug that changed color when filled with hot liquid. On either side of the Object Mobile, a platform opened to display an old Royal typewriter. I set chairs out so that passersby could sit down and type about the objects in their lives that were precious to them.

I liked the idea of creating an intersection where these conversations could happen. Since I'd already demonstrated an affinity for beautiful, ungainly, rolling creations, I roped my brother into yet another project (in postrecession Portland, he was one of many unemployed architects looking for work). I showed him my rudimentary sketches: a bicycle with a square box full of books attached. What if it could be a library on the street? What if it focused on people outside, instead of those who had easy access to an indoor library already? I knew from personal experience that there was nothing so powerful as a book to transport you from reality, to escape a particular circumstance for an afternoon. James was in. We would build a library and it would roll up into the squares, the fountains, the sidewalks of Portland, and it would serve a group of people who rarely got invited to anything, given their status as outsiders.

"You'll never see the books again."

That was a sentiment I heard more than once when I described the project to people, but I couldn't shake the idea of a street-level library.

Would I see the books again? There was only one way to find out.

UNQUALIFIED (BEN)

I kind of got suckered or blindsided, because going into a bar had been so far off my list for so long that I never considered it. I guess she got blindsided too, because she wasn't trying to stir up anything, she just accidentally got generous for a minute. I have no idea how a conversation broke out between us in the first place; I always kept to myself. She was at a sidewalk table and I was walking past, and we chatted for a while, and then out of politeness she offered to buy me a drink. It was too early in the day for me, and I said so, but out of politeness I agreed that a drink would be nice, so I went in with her, backpack and all. It was dreadful. She was just over halfway to the counter when the bartender started shaking his head. "No, you can't do this, these people, these unqualified people."

I wish I could say that I rose above it. That getting thrown out for being disgusting didn't bother me. That my only concern was for this poor child who only wanted to be my pal. That I had put my arm around her and said, "That's okay, honey, they just don't like our kind around here." That I didn't make a scene. I wish I could say that. But I saw that poor kid there, my pal, and I came up next to her and looked that bartender straight in the eye, just like Doc Holliday, and I spoke my piece.

"Not even a glass of water before I go, dearie? Oh, you're a scream. That is *sooo* Atlantic City."

Then I beat it through the door before they had a chance to finish throwing me out.

THE FIRST SHIFT (LAURA)

It was gray and misty the morning I pedaled the bike library on its maiden voyage. The Regional Arts & Culture Council had come through with a grant and I'd used part of the money to buy a used Haley Trike from Craigslist. It was a simple plywood box on wheels, but James had painted it a sea-blue color, added stained trim, and stenciled STREET BOOKS on each side. He'd also built a drawer inside that would pull out from the front, enabling me to display the books. To make sure it was level, James had set a bag of chicken feed inside it and taken it for a test ride in my neighborhood. It didn't tip over even when he took a sharp turn.

I carried titles I'd culled from my own shelves: *The Monkey Wrench Gang*, a copy of *Portland Noir*, and a handful of the Louis L'Amour westerns I'd inherited from my grandfather when he died. I'd also hit a used bookstore to stock up on some Stephen King, James Patterson, Nora Roberts, and others. Pedaling along, I watched for people with big backpacks or pieces of cardboard under them, sitting against buildings and in the doorways of businesses not yet open. As I kept an eye out for those who seemed weather-beaten, it struck me that I'd been conditioned for years to avert my eyes from people who were living outside, pushing a shopping cart, or just waking up on the sidewalk. Now I was doing the opposite: I actively looked for and hoped to find them.

FLYING SIGNS (BEN)

I wasn't crazy, exactly, but had a diminished capacity from depression. Sick is a good word for it, and creepy. Helpless, pathetic, contemptible—I was a regular walking thesaurus, a litany of mental health issues. Riding on the bus, trying not to sit too close to anyone, hunched inside myself as close as I could squeeze, which was completely ineffective as a prophylactic measure, but the best I could come up with under the circumstances. The first few weeks being outside, I suffered alienation from the people I'd left behind, as well as from the outdoorsmen I encountered on the streets. I was also paranoid. The man on the bus was not staring at me, but I was pretty sure he was.

Do we see a pattern emerging here? Let's review: I had finding-a-bathroom anxiety, riding-a-bus anxiety, finding-a-place-to-sleep anxiety, getting-a-seat anxiety, wet-feet anxiety. Most mental health professionals will confirm that depression and anxiety kind of go hand in hand. Some would agree that with serious long-term depression, psychosis is just around the corner (or was that it around the last corner?). I don't really understand that stuff. What I do know is that things can get pretty weird. But for those who are handling it well enough, being outdoors is not as pitiful as we fear it will be. One can adapt to nearly anything. One can also go nearly nuts from the shock of it before making the adjustment.

I wasn't one to fly a panhandling sign, but one I would have tried is:

> VIETNAM VET
> STILL CRAZY AFTER THAT ONE YEAR!

Found some sidewalk space up in the Pearl for a while. The sidewalks are just a little softer there, the spare change a little jinglier. But it turns out you have to bring designer cardboard with you, or the other homeless people look down on you. Imagine the snooty, nasal drone: "Frankly, it was embarrassing, the cardboard that THOOOSE PEEEOPLE were SLEEEEPING on!" Funny thought, that some of the homeless do look down on other homeless people. Must be some sort of basic human need, to be able to look down on someone. And homeless people serve an important function in society—we give everybody else someone to look down on. Maybe we should start charging for that. It was, in fact, the only sign I ever flew, for about ten minutes:

> FEEL SUPERIOR TO ME FOR FIVE MINUTES: 35¢
> ALL-DAY PASS: $3

Didn't get any change, but I did get a laugh.

> BE THE SPARE CHANGE
> YOU WANT TO SEE
> IN MY WORLD

Never flew that one either.

THE ROAD (LAURA)

As I passed by Skidmore Fountain, a firefighter named Fred, strawberry blond hair and freckles, leaned over the fence at the fire station and asked what I was doing.

"It's a street library," I said.

"How do you decide what books to offer?" he asked.

"I try to have a little bit of everything," I told him. "I understand that a man living outside might not want to unwind with a Jane Austen novel."

Fred grinned and leaned in closer. "I am *such* a fan of Jane Austen," he said. "Don't tell the guys here," and he hooked his thumb back toward the fire station, "but I've read every one of her books."

I had decided to use an old-school card and pocket system in each book, so people could sign the books out. I also had little Street Books cards to issue each person, on which I'd write their name and my location and hours.

The book bike was heavy on the uphill, and I was relieved when I arrived at the Park Blocks for the second library shift in Southwest Portland, near the art museum. I stopped under a canopy of trees to avoid the drizzle. Once the brakes were set, I pulled out the drawer and propped it up with a wooden block. Wiping raindrops from the books with a cloth, I took stock of my surroundings. The square drew many different kinds of people: scrappers with their skateboards and dogs on hemp leashes, gauges in ears, tattoos, pierced eyebrows, tongues, cheeks. A white-haired man, beard yellowed by nicotine, selling homemade wooden walking sticks. Guys with oversized backpacks at the north end of the square sat smoking and talking. The kids with dogs sprawled on the grass not far from me. People wandered through from the nearby farmer's market, carrying baguettes and flowers, leading small children or balancing on roller blades.

I confess I was nervous. What if nobody out here wanted a book? There was also a small voice in me that said, Really? A book? Somebody's been sleeping on a piece of cardboard on the concrete for months, and what you're going to offer is a paperback? It had occurred to me that a person who had been on the road for months or years might not enjoy reading *The Grapes of Wrath*.

My first patron wasn't a patron at all, but a security guard named AB. He studied my contraption, scanned the titles in the library, and then asked for my permit.

"I don't think I need a permit if I'm not selling anything," I told him.

He chewed on this information for a few minutes, circled the bike, and then shrugged. He rested his hand on the edge of the bike box and settled into a comfortable lean.

"I get notions to read stuff," he said. "Like books about secret government doings, and everything that we're not supposed to know." But he said he rarely finished a book before getting distracted, on account of his busy brain.

Just when I began to wonder if his uniformed presence at the library might hurt my business, he wished me luck and pushed off.

With AB gone, I screwed up my courage and approached the group of young people sprawled on the grass.

"Hey guys, I'm operating a library for people who live outside—you should come have a look at the books, if you'd like." I handed out a Street Books card to each person. Thomas was one of the first from the group to amble over and inspect my collection. Up close, I saw that he had sea-blue eyes that were both spooky and beautiful, and his chin and neck were tattooed with dark-blue designs.

"I take requests, if you have any," I said.

He studied me for a minute. "I've been meaning to read *Cold Mountain*, by Charles Frazier."

Whatever I might have supposed about a young man wearing mostly black, with tattoos on his face and neck, and gauges in his ears, it wasn't that he'd been meaning to read a retelling of *The Odyssey* set during the American Civil War. I realized I needed to keep my mind open and make no assumptions about what a patron might want to read, or about who they were. Nothing was a given. Each person was a walking secret history. It was up to them how much they revealed.

PEOPLE ARE STRANGE (BEN)

It wasn't written with spray paint—maybe it was nail polish. On the sidewalk near the Mission it read I NEED A BITCH WOT LIKES TO HAVE SEX. Of course I understood the sentiment. What guy doesn't? But I couldn't muster much sympathy for these frustrated yearnings, not feeling so hot myself. I lost count of the times I read that line on the sidewalk. Over on Couch Street, in front of the antique store, there's a crack in the sidewalk that, along with the right angle of the regular lines, makes it look a lot like the state of Idaho. Gave me something to look forward to while walking up the street.

I heard someplace that it's a symptom of schizophrenia when things take on a flat sort of appearance. Never was it so vividly portrayed to me as it was in the lyrics from The Doors, "Streets are uneven when you're down." Everything looks ugly, everyone is annoying, and it's a place you really don't want to be. I recommend avoiding it at all costs.

It wasn't catatonic schizophrenia or anything like that. But it was headed in that direction. A few flashes or weirdness, anyone gets that, but this came and went and left behind a dullness, and a knowledge that it doesn't matter how you got there, you got there for a reason and there is no way out. What you're left with is a whole lot of nothing every day, day in and day out. You get accustomed to not doing anything at all, in perpetuity, until something happens. And obviously nothing is going to happen while you're sitting there doing nothing at all. It was like a chain of events, but without any links in it. And I did that for three and a half years, because it was the best I could come up with on short notice.

THE SECOND SHIFT (LAURA)

The next week it was still misty and cool as I set the library up alongside Skidmore Fountain. There were police officers on horses posing for pictures with a gaggle of elementary school children. One kid could not get over the horses and kept reaching up as if to hug one around the neck, over the protestations of his teacher. After the students lined up and followed their teacher away, the officers roused a row of people along the fountain where they slept, hedged in by shopping carts covered in blue tarp, a tangle of clothing and bedding and arms. I watched as they groggily assembled their belongings. A young man in white stocking feet stared blankly at the bike library, and then went back to stuffing his gear into a plastic bag.

My first customer of the day was a man wearing red horn-rimmed glasses and a beard on the edge of feral. His hair grew just past his collar, and, were he to trade his shabby gray coat for a tweed jacket and his brown paper bag for a leather briefcase, it would have been easy enough to imagine him at the lectern of a university classroom. By now, the sun had burned off the mist, and the day was warm.

"Come have a look at these books," I said. "I'm running a free library. You check them out and then return them the next week, same time and place."

GQ (BEN)

At first, she looked like any other street librarian, complete with the cards in the books and Post-it Notes and paperclips. Bicycle parked, and little shelf pulled out, displaying the collection. I graciously overlooked the complete lack of any Wodehouse titles on her shelves, but did mention in passing that a well-maintained library does require some attention. Only too late would I learn that here was a teacher turned recalcitrant schoolchild that refuses to do her assigned reading. But I didn't know that yet.

I'd arrived in my ratty-looking coat. Scruffy beard. Hair going every which way, like I'd just stepped off the cover of *Gentlemen's Quarterly* and then into a threshing machine. The way I must have looked to Laura at the street library, it could easily have been straight out of Wodehouse. Describing one of Bertie's lovesick acquaintances, he writes, "He looked like a character in one of those Russian novels, trying to decide whether to murder several relatives before hanging himself in the barn."

TRAVELS WITH CHARLEY (LAURA)

The man in the glasses looked carefully through the titles, picking up a book and studying the back, then tucking it back onto the shelf.

"I wouldn't know whether to enlighten myself or just get something to kill the afternoon," he said.

I balanced a stack of paperbacks on the corner of the box and put a Street Books sticker on the bottom right cover of each one. Something told me that this person could be easily scared away if I gave him my full attention, so I busied myself with the books.

In the end, he chose Iain Levison's *Dog Eats Dog*, a satirical crime novel about a wounded bank robber who blackmails a history professor. He also checked out *Travels with Charley* by John Steinbeck. The former book lacked any mention of a real dog, but in the latter, Steinbeck's poodle is his travel companion. It's the story of an epic 1960 road trip in which Steinbeck and his dog go in search of America; Steinbeck describes the diners where he ate, and the conversations he had with everyday Americans. It also explores the ways it can be lonesome out on the road.

"I'm Laura," I said, and stuck out my hand.

The man shook it and said, "Ben Hodgson."

I wrote his name on the Street Books library card and gave it to him. "Okay then," he said. He gave a faint smile and a shrug, then turned and headed for the waterfront.

RECESS (BEN)

One morning, a man that worked at the downtown clinic I was sleeping outside of told me that it was time for me to move on. Somehow, after staying there three or four months without nobody saying a single thing to me, it struck me as a very reasonable request, and not at all like getting shoved around, so I went along peaceable-like. I went back to the Burnside Bridge for a few nights, then tried back at the closed-up Chinese food joint on Fourth, and that was when I noticed that the doorways on Third weren't always occupied. All I had to do was be the first one there, and since I got there early, right after dinner at the Mission, it was nothing at all to claim one of the spots for myself. I spent a little time in all three, and soon found my preferred spot. It had a little eight-inch recess in the wall that the others didn't, making it possible to stretch out all the way. The drawback was that the trash room for the apartment building was on the other side of the door, and a faint drift of sour garbage would get through occasionally.

I kind of got the routine of the place and looked around some. Found out about Musolf Manor, where three days a week, Father Dan provided a meals-on-wheels service to the tenants and brought enough extra for the homeless that lurked in the area. Sometimes he had sleeping bags, or shoes, or whatever. And five nights a week the Union Gospel Mission, the other Mission, had a dinner at eight. I added it up once. Instead of barhopping, you could go mealhopping. Be first in line at Blanchet at 5:30 p.m., then catch the tail end of it at the Rescue Mission, then be over at Musolf Manor about 7:45 p.m., and you could still get something at Union Gospel Mission before they closed. I think I actually did it once just to prove it.

Imagine you're the doorman at the bar. Now why in the hell would you go over to the guy in the doorway and hand him a ten-spot? I never knew. Now imagine you're the desk clerk at the Estate Hotel. Why would you go over to the guy in the doorway and warn him that the cops are going to move everybody so he'd better go, and besides, he's blocking the door to the garbage? I never knew that, either.

BRAVE NEW WORLD (LAURA)

Pretty soon I had help at the library. Celia had been in the high school writing class I taught at the art museum in the spring. I'd announced in our last class that I had gotten a grant to create a street library. I wasn't exactly sure what I was doing yet, but did anybody want to be an intern? It was crickets. But outside in the park, Celia ran up breathlessly behind me.

"I want to help you," she said.

It was the same with Sue, a freelance writer for *Street Roots*, a newspaper sold on street corners around the city by nearly two hundred vendors, many of whom lived outside. When she learned what I was doing with the bike library, she volunteered to help on the spot.

Each week my notebook filled with observations from the library shifts. I noted the man in a sweater cap with a grizzled gray beard who declined a book and said he was headed to see the navy ships. It was the start of the Portland Rose Festival, when giant ships eased into port and sailors spilled off onto the shore. At night, lights from the food booths and carnival rides reflected out over the green-gray Willamette River.

A man with a tattoo across the bridge of his nose checked out a James Patterson novel. A copy of Tom Robbins's *Still Life with Woodpecker* went to someone named Allen, and Loneheart had taken *Tales of Ordinary Madness*, the short story collection by Charles Bukowski. A girl with a shaved head named Rain told me stories about her six years in the juvenile justice system, where she'd studied Taoism and learned to pick locks. All her supposed mental illness was nothing more than diag-nonsense, she said. She checked out a copy of *Brave New World* and gave me a jaunty wave as she left the square.

As I got ready to close up, a man named Charlie stopped by. He wore a plain brown T-shirt with the sleeves cut off and a black bandana around his neck. Beard and tousled hair, smile lines etched at the corners of his eyes. I guessed he was in his forties, but it was hard to tell.

"Hello, sweetheart," he said, "whatcha got here?" He leaned over the library and studied the rows of books, then picked up my old copy of *The Monkey Wrench Gang*, by Edward Abbey.

"This book right here," he said, and held it to his chest. "This is a very big deal to the environmental movement, and it was important to his career." Charlie told me that back in college, he'd been assigned to accompany Abbey on a trip to the desert with a class, and to act as his assistant.

"But he got really drunk and drove away. He left us out there."

Charlie checked out the book, and when he signed his name, he wrote CHARLIE EAT IT! on the card.

"Do me a favor," he said.

"Yes?" I said.

"Have a wonderful day."

I watched him retreat, book tucked under one arm, hands stuffed into his pockets. There was no way to know whether the story he'd told me was true or not, but I decided it didn't matter. I'd read Abbey when I lived in Utah and remembered a quote from *Desert Solitaire* that I'd once underlined, about how a person could love and defend the wilderness without ever leaving the city. That even the idea of escape could give people hope and help them avoid "crime or drugs or psychoanalysis."

My last patron of the day was a young man named Nolan, who said that Charlie had told him about Street Books. His forehead was scuffed, and he showed me a wound on his hand. It had been a rough night. He checked out *Trask*, a novel by Don Berry about a mountain man exploring the wilds of the Oregon coast in 1848. Nolan was getting ready to hop a train north but said he'd return *Trask* when he passed back through. He put his hand to his heart.

"Thanks for doing this, sister," he said.

SORROWS (BEN)

I made it to the street library the next week and returned the books I'd taken the week before. I talked to Laura about *The Sorrows of Young Werther*, by Johann Wolfgang von Goethe. She pronounced his name right and everything. Werther *and* Goethe. The book was very popular, translated into every European language, and in its time, it had inspired a wave of suicides all over Europe. I'd learned that from the introduction of the book and had decided not to read it, because that was exactly what I didn't need. Instead, I checked out a little mystery novel, something about saving the galaxy, and an inspirational story about junkies who found Jesus. I sat at my customary spot a couple of benches down from the Steel Bridge and read my books there.

PERSUADER (LAURA)

By July, the sun had pushed the clouds away for good and it felt officially like summer. Children in flip-flops shrieked as they ran through the fountain at the waterfront. People stretched out on the grass, women in bikinis held magazines above their heads, men slept against their backpacks in the afternoon.

By then I'd fallen into a rhythm with the Street Books library, and I felt more confident about inviting people to check out books. Once they understood that there was no cost, and that the library was actually *for* them, people seemed to relax and peruse the selection. Some thanked me and said it was an important service I was offering. There was the occasional dissenter. Outside the art museum, a man hobbled past me in laceless shoes with a blanket over his shoulders. "I've already read everything there is," he said.

The more I went out with the bike library, the easier it was to interact with the public. I set up the library and let people come to me, trying to be friendly but leaving people alone who looked miserable or like they needed space. If someone said they weren't interested, I knew better than to feel stung about it.

On Wednesdays I parked the bike at Skidmore Fountain, where the MAX periodically rumbled through behind me. Ben Hodgson hadn't missed a shift since he'd stumbled onto the bike library a month before. He always returned his books and checked out more. One day he brought along a man he'd met down at the waterfront.

"This is Mike. He wants to read this," Ben explained, handing me the copy of *Persuader*, by Lee Child, that he'd checked out the week before. "But I told him he has to check it out from the library. You know, to make it official."

I looked at Mike. "Let's do it," I said.

Perhaps Mike had been sitting down by the waterfront a few minutes earlier, contemplating the shape his day might take. It was impossible to know his story unless he told it to me—all I had was my imagination. So, it was possible that the raw-knuckled girl sitting with the pink box of dumpster-dived Voodoo doughnuts had played clarinet in the school band when she was thirteen. Possible that she had once dreamed of being a figure skater or of riding steeplechase. What I couldn't see: her model horse collection, the wood carving of her name above her bed. I couldn't see the hopes her mother might have had for her. Or the lost baby teeth, or the red tennis shoes she'd loved, that she had eventually grown out of.

BATHROOM ETIQUETTE (BEN)

There are usually at least one or two people in line ahead of you at the Mission bathroom, or just about any of the available bathrooms in the area. The Rescue Mission asks people to observe a five-minute time limit whenever possible. Of course, some things take only about a minute or so, and a few things cannot be finished in only five minutes, so it gets tricky at times. You might see a guy go up and knock on the door, urging the present occupant to please hurry it up a little. I heard one guy plead, "C'mon, my back teeth are floating." And sometimes maybe the guy that is second in line wants to take cuts, and he will ask the guy that's first in line what his intended business is. Which is a very funny thing to see if you think about it. A grown man asking another grown man if he has to go number two. I never could bring myself to ask anyone if they had to poop. I'm not sure why. But this one guy came up with a fairly elegant solution to the dilemma. He used jailhouse slang, and very boldly and forthrightly asked the guy, "You dropping a deuce?" Which made it sound pretty cool, but you know what? I don't care how cool you make it sound, you've still just asked a grown man if he has to go number two.

Then there was the gentleman at the other Mission that wanted to take cuts ahead of me. He said he was only going to take a quick number one, and I didn't really want to let him take cuts, but his insistence won out, and in he went. And do you know what? He was in there a lot longer than it takes to do what he said he was going to do, and I immediately began to suspect that he was in there abusing some of his favorite substances. In fact, to this day I am still convinced.

GEEK LOVE (LAURA)

One day in the Park Blocks, a man named Luke skated up on his roller blades and paused to inspect the Street Books library titles. When he saw a copy of *Geek Love*, he said he used to be Katherine Dunn's neighbor and that he'd often heard the clack of her typewriter next door. Did I know about the mugging she'd fended off, he wondered? He said she'd coldcocked a woman who tried to grab her purse as she walked home with her groceries.

"She gave her a right hook," he said, "and then kept her down until police came." Luke was lanky, he was wearing glasses and a black sweatshirt with the hood up. He hung out with the crowd in the square at the Park Blocks, but when we spoke he mentioned his apartment, and in that way, I knew he had a roof.

Later, I bent over a Street Books library card to label it for a patron. "Remind me of your name?" I said.

"Genie with the Ten Foot Weenie!"

I remembered her from the week before, her eyes inked black with liner and the way she'd paced small circles during our conversation. She'd peered into my face and leaned close, causing me to rely on the technique I'd developed that summer: Whenever I felt the impulse to draw back or take flight, I'd flex the toes in one of my shoes. This helped me stand still to listen, to stay in one spot. Though I'd never once felt endangered, I'd occasionally have some very strange conversations, and the toe flex worked every time.

Genie said she loved the Street Books project so much that she wanted to contribute something. That's why she'd gathered all of the books from the lounge inside her apartment complex and brought them to me in her arms, breathless and eyes wild because her landlord had chased her part of the way.

HIDING INSIDE A BOOK (BEN)

Things was crashing in on me. Dehydration, then sore shoulders. All the inaction, the sedentary lifestyle, it was starting to sink in. One thing you never see is homeless guys doing calisthenics. I got so stiff in the joints that taking my jacket off and putting it back on was a major production, some kind of twelve-step process.

Was I depressed and freaked? Well, if you can't talk to anyone, or barely even look at anyone, there must be something wrong somewhere. Standing in the dinner line at the shelter, I would bring a book with me so I could hide my face and not have to interact.

BLINDNESS (LAURA)

It was late July and Charlie said he gave the copy of *The Monkey Wrench Gang* to an autistic kid.

"He's good for it," he said. It was an overcast Wednesday morning at Skidmore Fountain.

He checked out *Blindness* by José Saramago and left the card with another CHARLIE EAT IT! when he signed out.

A patron named Terry requested stories about champions, about characters who transcended the challenges in their lives to become winners.

"*Seabiscuit* is a book about a horse judged by the way it looked," Terry said, "but there was a man who saw some capability in that horse, and a light. People didn't recognize the heart that the horse had."

I guessed Terry was in his thirties. He had tousled dark hair and expressive brown eyes. This was the second week in a row we'd crossed paths, and I saw he had a shy, gentle quality about him.

Clint, who was sixteen and staying at the Harbor Light Center, asked me if he qualified for the Street Books library, since he wasn't technically sleeping on the actual street.

"Of course you do," I said.

Sleeping in a car, in a shelter, on a friend's couch—all of this meant living at the margins and a lack of access to services those of us in secure housing take for granted. He checked out *A Million Little Pieces* by James Frey. Debra, also young, was combing through the library, searching for a book.

She pointed at Clint's selection. "Just so you know, that guy made up a bunch of stuff in his memoir. It's not actually all true."

Clint shrugged. "If it's a good story, it doesn't matter so much."

"It *does* matter," Debra said. "I was totally into it, and only halfway through when I heard he'd made it all up. He pretended to be this badass who kicked drugs all by himself, but it was a lie. It sucked to find that out!"

"But if it's one hundred percent true and boring, who's gonna read it?" Clint said.

I listened as two teenagers suddenly engaged in a debate about an author's responsibility to tell the truth when it comes to penning a memoir, the subjectivity of "truth," and the necessity of some invention whenever one is constructing stories from the past. The writing teacher part of me wanted to pump my fist in the air and say, "Yessss!"

Ben Hodgson appeared and eventually checked out a James Patterson book, but we talked about Jack London.

"He really lived it," Ben said. "He didn't have to make it up."

TIME SLOWS DOWN (BEN)

If you want to get a shower at the drop-in center at TPI (Transition Projects), you can show up early and wait for an hour until they open the doors, or you can show up any old time and wait for an hour in the line for your turn to come. Either way, it takes a whole extra hour. You don't have to change clothes, but if you decide to, there's a line for that.

Street time runs very slow. Nobody carries an appointment calendar. Not germane to the situation. If you had the most expensive pocket planner on the market, you couldn't even get a five-dollar crack hit for it at the bus station. For these guys, just getting to the next page, the one called tomorrow, is an all-day project. And that's only for the ones that are still able to function, which would not have included me. I was so caught in a loop that even making it across the Burnside Bridge was like heading up the Orinoco in a rowboat.

THE DOORS OF PERCEPTION (LAURA)

One afternoon I met Jesus, or at least a man whose hair, bare feet, and general demeanor reminded me of the stories of Jesus I'd grown up with. He told me he liked to live lightly on the earth, and that he tried not to consume any more resources than he absolutely had to. His hands were unwashed but steady as he sorted through his collages, showing me pages of intricate images woven together, bursts of color, and scripture from the book of Revelation. It was the sort of conversation I might have had with an artist in a studio, and yet, I figured there must have been a psychiatric label someone would apply to this person.

I had many conversations like this at the Street Books library, where I'd gradually be drawn into the story of someone who seemed quite stable, and then suddenly they would mention the millions of tiny antennae we have on our skin, how they are attuned to everything around us and we just have to pay attention. My skin would crawl a little and I'd wonder if I was afraid or if it was the antennae and I'd just never been aware of them before. The conversation with a man named David followed a similar pattern. He rode up on a silver ten-speed and stopped to gaze into the book bike.

"Wow," he said. "What a neat idea you've got here. Just neat." He shook his head in wonder. He was tall and lean, with a face reddened from the alcohol he said he'd quit two years earlier. I asked him how he'd done it, and he said prison helped.

"How long have you been out?" I asked.

"Well, I'm glad you asked." He rubbed his chin and then cupped it. "But it's a tricky question." He described how he'd recently realized that he'd been living for several years inside the space of each year, so that there had been a kind of compression to time. This meant that even though he'd only been out of prison for two or three years, it was actually more like six in real-life years. He said that his mother had called to wish him a happy anniversary at the one-year mark of being out of prison.

"But that was years ago now," he said.

David shared a number of interesting theories with me. For example, aspartame was a combination of nuclear waste and E. coli.

"We have Donald Rumsfeld to thank for that," he said.

I wrote ASPARTAME=RUMSFELD in my notebook.

He said he was alive and awake now. Everything felt possible. He said, "We have to wake up!" and I felt a shiver of recognition. My favorite quote by the writer Aldous Huxley was, "Our business is to wake up." It's what my friend Beck from high school had painted on my bedroom wall in hopes that I'd be her psychedelic companion and try LSD with her (I'd been too timid at the time).

David said he'd quit his job, given away all his belongings except for the bicycle. No more junk food, drinking, or smoking. Now that he was on the road, he was all lightness.

"I'm going to Sedona," he said.

"Sedona?" I said. "What's there?"

He grinned. "The desert."

ONE DAY IN THE LIFE (BEN)

One day I was on my bench by the Steel Bridge, reading *One Day in the Life of Ivan Denisovich*. It's about a sovietski prisoner doing a ten-year stretch at a work camp in the Siberian hinterland. At the end of his day, and the book, he adds up the things that went right, and the things that could have gone wrong, but didn't. He declares it a pretty good day. The reader is supposed to be horrified that anyone would call the day he described a "good" day, but I guess I must have misunderstood. I was thinking what a lucky bastard he was. At least he had a social life, and here I was stuck on my damn bench.

*

BREAKFAST OF CHAMPIONS (LAURA)

Ajax was camped under the Burnside Bridge and left his sleeping pad to come and see the library. He checked out *Dreams from My Father*, by Barack Obama, and smiled with the handful of teeth he had left.

"I'm just sorry that Michelle Obama and Princess Diana couldn't have been friends," he said. "What a pair that would have been, you know?"

"Why's that?" I asked.

"Well, you know, both of them were very regular people stuck in a formal environment. I mean, they had to send their people out just to get a hamburger!"

Other patrons gathered around the bike. Randy asked for writing about Islamic Jihad and anything on Jungian psychology. Mike checked out a book by Kurt Vonnegut. Stephanie took a Nora Roberts novel called *Sacred Sins*.

Eric was another regular. A diminutive Marlboro Man with his Wranglers, cowboy boots, and walking stick. This week he wore a baseball hat with a ONE WAY sign on it, pointing to the word JESUS. He stuck his tongue out at me as he'd done since the very first time I'd met him, and greeted me in his customary way, "How you doing kiddo?" He had his eye on my grandfather's Louis L'Amour novels.

Beer Change the Pirate (not his given name) came by for a second week. I knew that he was a veteran and that he'd had all his belongings stolen earlier in the summer.

He showed me the treasures in his pocket and said he'd just come from a game of random pocketry.

"Random pocketry?" I asked.

"Random pocket *trade*," he said.

He told me that the rules consisted of each person reaching inside their pocket and pulling out an item, which they then handed over to the other without looking.

"That's basically it," he said. "The rules." In his grimy palm he displayed a pocketknife, some twine, cigarette rolling papers, and a chunk of green malachite. The traveler's stone. Something with good properties to keep one safe on a journey.

STANFORD'S (BEN)

Once a month, Stanford's Restaurant came in with a meal, which was a real treat for the Mission-goers. I wish I could be there on a Stanford's night on the very same night some guy goes homeless for the first time; he's gonna think, "Damn, I should have left home sooner—this is great." See how long it takes for him to realize he's been had. Something similar did actually happen to me on one of my very first visits. It wasn't a Stanford's night, but definitely one of the better meals: fried chicken. Usually, it's about a thousand and one ways to ruin a pasta dish. The sad truth is that it has to be that way, with the substandard fare. If you take away the long line and make the food too tasty, everybody would want to eat there, and the down-and-outers would get shoved off to the side.

RAW FOOD (LAURA)

I got an email from Beth Chapman, a librarian with a Master's in library/information studies from Berkeley. She said she'd seen an article in the *Oregonian* about Street Books and wanted to get involved. When I explained that I was not a professional librarian and this was not a traditional library, she was not fazed. Put me to work, she said.

In short order, she became the onsite reference librarian at the Park Blocks shift each Saturday. In a conversation about books, a patron might say, "I loved his first book, but I can't remember the second one in that series. That's the one I want." We'd turn to Beth, who would perform a magical search on the smartphone she'd pulled from her pocket and produce the answer. I'd scribble it down in my notebook, and we'd do our best to get the book for the following week.

Mattias, a teenager who had very recently transitioned off the streets and into an apartment, was interested in organic gardening. Someday, he told us, he was going to be an organic gardener and live on a piece of land outside the city. In the meantime, he wanted to read a book about raw foods. That week, Beth found a copy of a raw foods cookbook on sale at Powell's, complete with full color pictures of beet salads and carrot juice.

The next week she brought the book to the library shift. I wrote HOLD FOR MATTIAS on a piece of paper and stuck it on the front of the book. He didn't show. The following week, as we stood alongside the bike library, a man perused the selection and tucked several books under his arm. I watched him flip through the raw foods book and add it to his growing collection.

Beth's eyes widened. I returned her look: That was *Mattias's* book.

But we hadn't seen Mattias. Not for two weeks now. How long would we hold a book before releasing it back into the library's collection? Clearly, we needed a policy.

"What do you charge for your books?" the man asked.

"There's no charge," I said. "We're a street library, and we focus on people who live outside and might not be able to access the mainstream library."

He smiled. "I am not outside . . . yet. But I am this close." He held his thumb and forefinger together, nearly touching.

"Can I ask where you're from?" By his accent, I guessed it was somewhere in the Middle East.

He smiled again. Gaunt, large brown eyes. "I'll give you a hint: Your country is currently dropping bombs on it."

"Uh, you'll have to be more specific," I said. "That could be a lot of places right now."

In the end, he departed with a short stack of books, including the raw foods cookbook. I hadn't had the heart or nerve to try and talk him out of it, and the next week, Beth returned to Powell's and got another copy. We waited for Mattias the following week, and then the week after that. But he never came.

APHORISM (BEN)

It was one dull day after another. By then I had found a few different places to find cardboard, and I'd be spreading it out there in front of the downtown clinic, and I'd have to read the set-in-the-pavement quotation: THEY ALWAYS SAY TIME CHANGES THINGS, BUT YOU ACTUALLY HAVE TO CHANGE THEM YOURSELF. I got tired of seeing it; it got to be like a taunt. I suppose what Warhol said was true enough, in the way that it was intended, but from a mental health standpoint it doesn't fly. That is, there is no such thing as some supreme effort of will that can make depression go away. When you're down you're down, and you ain't getting back up, especially if you're living outside.

ALL-AMERICAN POEM (LAURA)

By late August, I was accustomed to greeting my regular patrons as well as curious passersby who stopped to investigate the library. One day, identical men in plaid shirts and horn-rims walked up. I realized they were Matthew and Michael Dickman, the twin poets who had grown up in the Lents neighborhood in Southeast Portland. They admired the books and offered to donate poetry of their own, if we could use it, then headed off on their way. Since they were coming from the farmer's market, one of them carried baguettes, the other a bag of giant pickles.

Scarlett was there the same day. By then she'd burrowed through all of the *Twilight* books, exchanging one fat tome for the next until she'd read them all. When she returned Stephanie Meyer's final book, she requested a book on pregnancy.

"Congratulations," I said.

Scarlett wore her hair dyed an electric magenta and she smiled and ducked her head. "Thank you."

"How are you feeling these days?" I jotted a line in my notebook: FIND A COPY OF WHAT TO EXPECT WHEN YOU'RE EXPECTING FOR SCARLETT.

"Not bad," she said. "The nausea was pretty bad with the cigarettes."

"I can imagine." I straightened the Street Books sign on the bike. "I suppose it's just as well to quit for now."

"Actually, I just switched to menthols and that's been helping." She stepped back and did a tiny wave. "See you next time."

FLOWCHART (BEN)

I came across a small green-gray backpack in a very unlikely spot. Not on the sidewalk, but if you looked over the railing down to the public driveway, still left out in the open. Hidden, but poorly hidden. A programmer could draw up a flowchart for the ethical dilemma, the questions being the diamond-shaped decision boxes: (1) Is the rightful owner coming back to retrieve his or her property? (2) Is this property still going to be here when he or she comes back? (Obviously not, if I take it.) (3) Maybe I'd better steal it before someone else does?

I went down and picked it up, and among other things that I found in the bag was a screw jack. It left me a little puzzled, why anybody would carry a screw jack around, until I mentioned it to an experienced guy that I knew. "You can pop a bike lock with one of those." This cleared up a couple of things. Evidently the rightful owner thought it prudent to ditch the thing before he got picked up. I gave myself a pass to help myself to the property, reasoning that there wasn't much of a chance at all that it would have still been there by the time the guy got out of jail. Honor among thieves and returning a burglar's tools to their rightful owner only counts for so much.

A REQUEST (Laura)

AB, the security guard from my very first shift that June, the one who'd asked to see my permit, stopped by the Park Blocks shift most weeks to say hello. He said that he occasionally encountered our patrons waiting in the square with a book to return, or someone with a sack of books they wanted to donate. If they had missed us, or were standing there on the wrong day, AB would let them know when they should come back to find us. In this way, he became an unlikely—and uniformed—spokesperson for the street library. When I offered to bring him any book he'd like, he requested one called *The Unseen Hand*.

Virgil was a wiry, restless character who was never still. He was tan, with a gray goatee, and often appeared at the library shifts wearing a bandana tied over his head. He had scars: one that ran from his cheekbone to the edge of his mouth, and one along his rib cage that he lifted his T-shirt to show me. By late summer, he became a kind of self-appointed security detail for the street library. He didn't elaborate, but whatever he'd done as a younger man had resulted in more than two decades in prison. Now, he was a thoughtful street philosopher, solicitous and anxious to help. He showed me a dumpster in Old Town that often held bags of artisanal bread.

Virgil was one of several patrons featured in a documentary film by Travis Shields that came out later that year.

When Shields asked him what sort of books he liked to read, Virgil confessed that he was considering giving up reading books for a while.

"I've read so much I'm worn out," he said. "I know too much. I gotta let my doing catch up to my knowing."

He was in the middle of reading *The Book of Five Rings* by samurai warrior Miyamoto Musashi when someone stole his backpack and bicycle. The book is a manual on martial arts that's also full of principles that can be applied to everyday life. Virgil had called on what he'd learned from Musashi to stay calm and to do slow circles, first one block, then two, then three, fanning out until he found his bicycle stashed in an alley. His backpack was gone, along with a U-lock and the copy of the nearly five-hundred-year-old book, but it was still a victory to climb on his bicycle and ride away.

STEALTH TAG (BEN)

Started to get used to the pace of it, irritants and all. The weekends were merciless with the noise and the rowdies. Why is it funny to say "WAKE UP" to a guy that's trying to sleep? Well, because it is. It's almost as funny as kicking the guy, so your friends can see what a great sense of humor you have. And besides, it is too funny. I could see myself doing that. The thing is, it wasn't a real kick. He pulled the punch so well that it didn't amount to much more than a love tap. Gave his friends a good laugh, and his girlfriend didn't even think he was that much of an asshole.

If that guy lacked stealth, the next guy did not. One morning, as I was rolling up my yellow sleeping bag, I saw the writing on it. I had gotten tagged during the night. The miscreant(s) showed good taste though. The midnight-blue spray paint looked good on the yellow bag. Really stood out.

The weeknights were quieter, and the population would get sparse well before closing time. Plenty of chances to hit the can. One night, I was only a tree or two down, and the sixty seconds with my back turned was long enough to get raided. Some wanderer that needed something came by and found it. Only the blanket was gone, not the sleeping bag.

The outdoorsmen's crowd is an amorphous one that moves around from place to place, sometimes in reaction to enforcement, which in turn is sometimes reacting to the crowds. I never figured it out and maybe no one really knows.

There's no sense to it. At the Skidmore MAX stop there's a strip of sidewalk that's been alternately occupied and cleared out three or four times. They cleared it out the last time in reaction to a stabbing, which is logical. If they had done nothing, and all the same people stayed there, something as bad or worse could happen a few days later and they'd be on the hook for acting like they didn't even care. Now it's been over a year and it's still off-limits, possibly because no one wanted them there in the first place. It's also possible that if it did make any sense, it wouldn't be the government. Some people think the homeless get singled out by the cops. I figure it's just because we are so visible and so ubiquitous, and it's the ubiquity that draws all the attention.

THE UNSEEN HAND (LAURA)

Virgil and I talked while we pushed the bike uphill to the Park Blocks. The plan was to set him up with the library, and he would run the last hour of the shift so I could go see my son's soccer game. As we walked, he told me he'd had a recent bit of trouble. He wasn't one hundred percent sure, but maybe there was a warrant out for his arrest.

"Are you sure you want to set up in a public place and draw attention to yourself?" I asked him.

He cracked the knuckles on both hands as we walked. Rangy, restless.

"Yeah yeah, I'm sure. I gave you my word I'd do this, so don't worry about me."

When we got there, he hustled to pull out the drawer and hang the sign, and we were open for business. I liked that he took pains to greet patrons by their names if he knew them. And that those he didn't know were welcomed and introduced to the library.

I noticed AB in his uniform and bike helmet from across the square and waved at him. I had found a used copy of A. Ralph Epperson's *The Unseen Hand* at the Powell's on Hawthorne. It was subtitled *An Introduction to the Conspiratorial View of History*, and I wondered if I was imagining things when the bookseller gave me a quizzical look.

A crowd formed around the library, and I was kept busy checking out books. When there was a break between patrons, Virgil pulled me aside and pretended to ask a question about the card catalog system. In a quiet, measured voice, he said, "There's a cop over there scoping me, so I'm taking a walk. I've put my wallet and ID in your bag so I don't lose them, in case I need to disappear." He took off without looking back and walked across the park.

I glanced up to see AB leaning against his bicycle. "How you doing, Miss Laura?" he said. "Any chance you found my book?"

The cop that was "scoping" Virgil had come to pick up his request.

"As a matter of fact, I do have your book," I said.

SHOPPING (BEN)

"I wish my food card would turn back on. I'm tired of steal-ing stuff." Lucky said that once.

I heard about a girl who would make three or more trips to the supermarket a day. She never took much, just a little something to snack on. It was her version of what everyone else calls standing in front of the refrigerator.

We were just about at the end of our rope, and some ass-hole had greased the last few feet of it.

LORD OF THE FLIES (LAURA)

When the Occupy Wall Street movement hit New York City that fall, activists in Portland took over a block on SW Main Street, settling in Lownsdale and Chapman Squares. College students, retirees, anarchists, professors, and activists set up tents, a community kitchen, and even planted kale in the soil. While the media provided breathless hourly coverage of the Occupy movement, a different kind of encampment popped up on the corner of NW Fourth and Burnside. Right next door to the giant lion statues guarding the gate to Portland's Chinatown, a group of people who had been living outside had come together and formed a community. By the time the city and police took notice of them, they were settled in.

I pieced together the story from newspaper articles. The vacant corner lot was owned by a man named Michael Wright, who had operated an adult bookstore in that spot until 2007, when the city deemed the building to be unsafe, and demolished it. Wright applied for a permit from the city to open up the now-empty lot to food carts, but was told that he could not set up food carts on the gravel. When he applied for a permit to put in a cement slab, he was informed that doing so would turn the site into a parking lot, which violated the moratorium on new parking lots in the city center. So, Wright was stuck. Maybe he would "donate it to Dignity Village for a year," he threatened in a *Portland*

Tribune article. Enter Leo Rhodes and Ibrahim Mubarak, housing activists with the nonprofit Right 2 Survive. Before moving to Portland, Rhodes had been an advocate for numerous tent cities in Seattle, and Mubarak was the cofounder of Dignity Village, a self-governed community located on a city-owned industrial lot out by the airport. So yes, they had some ideas about how to use the space. Wright leased the corner lot to them for one year, for the cost of one dollar, thereby following through on his "threat." Mubarak christened the encampment Right 2 Dream Too (or R2D2), and the word spread. People began to arrive with their backpacks and bedding. In short order, volunteers from the community installed a fence made of old doors they'd found at the Re-Building Center, creating a privacy screen along Burnside, the city's main east–west artery downtown. Soon, the rest area featured a check-in/security desk, rows of tents, and an outdoor kitchen where donated bread and fruit were stored. Eventually there was even a makeshift computer lab and small vegetable garden. For the residents of R2D2, it meant a secure place to store gear while leaving for treatment or applying for jobs. It meant not carrying or pushing their belongings around all day. It meant that no police officer would prod them awake in the middle of the night and tell them to move on.

The space accommodated between sixty and seventy people per night, free of charge. They adhered to a strict set of governing principles that included a no drug/alcohol policy, and they conducted litter patrols up and down the block. Though many neighboring businesses were less than thrilled about having a group of people camping in a nearby lot, there were no calls to the police during that time related to the rest area, and the encampment gradually became a part of the community in Chinatown. I began to stop there on Wednesdays on my way to Skidmore Fountain, and I quickly got to know the residents. Gordon liked books about sports. Mama Chewy was in the middle of the *Harry Potter* series, and Marckus loved Jackie Collins's romance novels.

A small man named P2P played the ukulele for me one day, out on the sidewalk near the tents. He told me that he wanted to request children's books and books about cooking, but that he wasn't a very strong reader.

"I'm one of the mentally retarded," he said.

I wondered who in his life had told him that. A teacher? His mother? A guidance counselor? *One of the mentally retarded* sounded like a label someone had stuck to his shirt years before that he'd worn ever since. Mark Hubble, another resident, told me about meeting Ray Bradbury as a child, and how the author was the most famous person he'd ever met. He said I should read the collection of stories called *The Illustrated Man*. In "Kaleidoscope," Mark's favorite story, astronauts are floating through space after their craft malfunctions, communicating with each other via helmet speakers, and knowing their deaths are imminent. The narrator reflects on the time he realizes he has wasted. "Is there anything I can do now to make up for a terrible and empty life?" he wonders. As he enters the atmosphere, he's incinerated. Down on earth, a boy in Illinois looks up and screams, "Look, Mom, look! A falling star!" His mother tells him to make a wish.

One day during a shift at R2D2, I put a sticker on a copy of William Golding's *Lord of the Flies*. I'd read the book in high school and remembered that Golding puts forth the idea that a group of young people, left to their own devices on a remote island, would revert to savagery. The existence of the folks at R2D2 struck me as a compelling argument against Golding's assumption. These were people who'd taken the scant resources they had in common and forged a successful community. Sure, they weren't on a desert island, and they weren't children, but in many ways they'd embarked on a similar kind of experiment. A diverse community of people whose common denominator was a lack of shelter had come up with their own rules by which to govern themselves. I knew it would be naive to assume that everything ran smoothly all the time there. But that day, as I set the book out on display, I decided that William Golding might be pleasantly surprised to see the kind of society being constructed at Right 2 Dream Too.

SHELL GAME (BEN)

I had company for a few weeks. A guy named Gordon that I sort of marginally knew was caught in the same sweep as me at Burnside and showed up the same night I did. He was about my age and knew the same sports, and we'd talk briefly now and then. He moved on when the Right to Dream opened for business. I didn't think Right to Dream was going to last, and I never moved in there. This was about the same time the Occupy movement had moved into town, and the city's enforcement arm was focused on them for several months, by which time the people at R2D2 had firmly established themselves. So, I guess we could say that the Occupy protesters did accomplish at least one thing. By the time the authorities finally made the crowd leave City Hall, Right to Dream had publicity and widespread support. After that, it became this shell game, where the city would propose a new location for the camp, then the neighborhood associations would fight it. Smart money was on the existing camp being a fixture right where they were for a good three to five years, especially with the new distraction of the housing emergency and the other new camps springing up. Citywide, nationwide, worldwide. A Swedish guy named Olaf told me that they are out there on the streets of Stockholm. They got 'em in Tokyo too. Then there was the Somali dude at the Mission that said, "In Somalia, everybody is homeless."

AUTUMN (LAURA)

The morning air was crisp in late September, so I pedaled the bike library with my hands tucked into the sleeves of my sweater. I was seeing fewer patrons as the weather got cooler, but our regulars still showed up every week. Keith was leaning against the concrete of Skidmore Fountain when I arrived, and he gave a two-finger salute from his brow. What I knew about Keith after a summer of lending books to him: He was a veteran and kept himself impeccably neat. Beard trimmed, backpack and bedroll cinched tight. He wore a dangling silver cross in one ear and a cap with a brim. He lived in Forest Park, where he'd found a spot deep off the trail and could rely on nobody messing with his campsite.

Each week he would return two books and check out two new ones. His favorite genres were science fiction, military history, and mysteries. He never lingered long at the library. Just perused the selection and chose his two books. That day, when he departed, he said, "Thanks, Laura. See you next week." As I watched him go, I realized suddenly that this was no longer the three-month art project I'd originally conceived, no longer something that fit neatly into the warm months before being boxed up and taped closed. Most every shift began with at least one patron waiting for me. Sometimes it was a small crowd. Where would they return their books if I disappeared? Where would they find new books to read? I had to keep the library running.

WHIRLPOOL (BEN)

Maybe there is a perfectly good reason to whirlpool into despondency. Maybe it is because it's much easier to take than the humiliation that comes when you first end up outside. At first I was confused, a little paranoid, unsure of myself. Then, as I gradually took stock of my situation, which was bleak—not being indoors any longer, having no place to hide it, like here-is-a-complete-idiot-for-all-the-world-to-see—slinking off into unknown doorways is a fairly rational way to numb off any kind of feeling. At least no one has to watch.

DOWN AND OUT
IN PARIS AND LONDON (LAURA)

Ben Hodgson waited until the patron ahead of him was finished checking out a book before making his approach. This week he had no jokes. In fact, he was more dispirited than I'd ever seen him.

"How's it going, fine sir?" I asked.

He shrugged and turned his attention to the books.

Up close I saw how threadbare his jacket was. It occurred to me that it was literally coming apart at the seams.

"It's getting pretty chilly. Have you looked into a coat upgrade for the winter?"

He shook his head and said, "I had three different opportunities to go to coat drives in the past week, and I just didn't make it to any of them."

"Why do you think you're being so hard on yourself?" I asked. "Why not get a coat?"

He shook his head again. "Despair is actually the most deadly sin," he said. "Worse than all the others—greed, avarice, all of that." He gestured at the library. "I think I read that in one of these books."

He handed me two books. "These will do."

I removed the cards from inside each cover. While he signed them out, I studied the covers.

"You didn't exactly go with escapist reads here," I told him. "This Orwell is kind of a downer, and *No Country for Old Men* is an intense one. Cormac McCarthy can be bleak."

He tucked the books under his arm. "I gotta get out of here," he said. "All this introspection is bringing me down."

QUESTION FOR LAURA (BEN)

Q: Do you know what the homeless guy's dog was thinking?

A: Wow, this is the longest walk we've ever been on.

THE COAT (LAURA)

That week I went against my own rules and bought Ben a coat at Goodwill. I hadn't figured out what I would say to him when I presented it, and I hoped he wouldn't be offended. But it was too cold to be sleeping outdoors without better insulation from the cold. It was a good coat. Fleece-lined and waterproof. The next week, I folded it in half and tucked it in the box on top of the books. I waited for him at Skidmore Fountain, but he never appeared. It was the same the following week and the week after that. It was beginning to be a pain to operate the library while working around the coat. Sue gently suggested that we might want to stick to what we did best: lending books. I gave the coat away to someone else, but I didn't stop looking for Ben. Each week I remained hopeful and each week he didn't show.

TWO

ROUTINE (BEN)

When the first season came to a close and the cold weather began closing in, I discovered the public library as a way to beat the cold during the day. Soon, I developed a routine. Breakfast at the Mission, go up to the Julia West House, get to the library as soon as it opened, back to the Mission for dinner, then retire for the evening. I always took care to avoid all puddles, which can be challenging in Portland.

I had this industrial strength trash bag, and I'd get up around six, bag up my stuff, roll a cigarette, and head to the Mission. The idea was to get in and out early, so when I got up to the Julia West House, I could get one of the better seats. Then I'd time it right and crowd the door when the library opened, so I could get my favorite seat in there. I was still, for the most part, a mental case, and my day consisted of accruing small meaningless advantages like that. I'd leave the library and go back to the Mission for dinner, then back to the sidewalk.

By the time the next Street Books season started, my habits were so ingrained that I was never around when the book bike was out.

LIFE CYCLE (LAURA)

How do you keep an art project alive after it's lived beyond its original plan? I didn't know for sure, but experience had taught me that the community generally rallied behind a creative idea, especially if it seemed like it was for a good cause. With the help of Sue and Beth, I cobbled together a Kickstarter campaign and we launched it in mid-September.

The Mercy Corps Action Center at Skidmore Fountain had allowed me to store the bike library during the summer when I wasn't using it to deliver books. They also let us use the space to hold our first reception in September, marking the end of the season and inviting the public to come and learn about Street Books. In the weeks before the reception, I spread the word to all our patrons about the event.

Eric, our Marlboro Man patron who loved Louis L'Amour was there. So was Keith with his neat backpack and cross earring. A food cart agreed to cater and arrived with white tablecloths and very fine finger foods. It was the first event I ever held for Street Books and I knew it might be unwieldy and hard to predict how it would go with the mix of people living outdoors alongside people who had driven from their homes to come and see what was going on. But the backpacks and gear were stashed away, and people ate together and visited amiably. For a while, it wasn't obvious who would return to a house later that evening and who would head back to an encampment under a bridge.

We asked for $4,000 and when the campaign ended and Kickstarter took their cut, we ended up with slightly more than that amount.

Not long after that, a friend sent me a link with the message, "I sure hope you're applying for this." It was an application for the Innovations in Reading Prize from the National Book Foundation. It felt like a long shot, but I applied on behalf of Street Books and then forgot about it. I took a break after the September event at Mercy Corps, but by October I was back outside, connecting with some of the patrons I'd worked with in summer and meeting some new ones. November, December, a break for the holidays, and then back out in it for January.

DROPOUT (BEN)

I already knew about TPI. I had looked in the window once, and a roomful of bunk beds looked about as appealing as the county jail. I was better off living in my car. Two years later, the car was long gone, and the dread of winter was enough to make TPI start looking like a good idea. For some, it's a safety net that works just like it's supposed to. They get the maneuvering room they need and never do get stuck outside. Others come in off the street and make it out for good. Some, me among them, go back out no better off than they came in, with nothing more to show for it than the experience. I overheard one of the counselors explaining to a colleague why you take the good with the bad and don't worry too much about failing to reach the unreachable. "Everybody's got their own demons."

Meaning, I suppose, that the laws of conformity can't possibly offer a one-size-fits-all approach to those outside the mainstream. My biggest demon at the time was having to be there, and it did cross my mind that the winter weather might have been easier to take than being around people. I had gotten to the point where I was wondering who the dropout was, me or the system. One guy managed to get a different bunk when someone moved out. That's extra work for the staff, and he was asked how he managed it. "It depends who you ask," he explained, "and how you ask." The rare sharpster who knew something about how systems work, and how to work them to your own advantage. Bide your time, pick your spot, and come in under the radar.

There were some lockers on a back wall, big enough to hold a change of clothes and a toothpick maybe, so people had to keep their stuff on the floor or hanging off their bunks. It was so crowded that going out during the day didn't take much incentive.

SMALL MIRACLE (LAURA)

I was finishing up my shift, biking the library through Skidmore Fountain—it was kind of a lonesome, blustery day, freezing outside and gray—and all of a sudden I heard someone yell, "Hey Book Lady!" It was Pamela, a patron I'd gotten to know over the summer who often traveled with a giant shopping cart laden with blankets and plastic bags and pictures of her kids.

"Have you got my poetry?" she asked.

And I did. I had two volumes of poetry marked PAMELA. *Ultramarine* by Raymond Carver and a collection of Gwendolyn Brooks poems. I'd been carrying them for a month, looking for her all over Old Town Chinatown, and suddenly there she was.

POCKETS <small>(BEN)</small>

As the saying goes, "If a pickpocket meets a holy man, he sees only his pockets." This is not so much a value judgment on the relative merits of holy men and pickpockets, but more a psychological observation about how motivation affects perception.

I've often wondered how to justify my thieving ways. One of the saints, Thomas Aquinas or maybe Augustine, argued persuasively that stealing is morally justifiable for the very poor, although I am not sure that lifting a Hershey's with almonds from the Plaid Pantry is included in the list of exceptions. Fortunately, I worked hard to obtain an advanced degree in applied metaphysics, even spending an entire semester dissecting Spinoza's *Situational Ethics*, paying particular attention to the chapter on not getting caught.

FAMILY DRAMA <small>(LAURA)</small>

The kids were outside my bedroom door. I could hear them whispering, their footfalls disappearing and returning. When I opened the door, I saw they'd left me something on the floor. A piece of paper folded into a kind of box with the message: HELP NEDID AND MUNNY NEDED. There was one penny inside.

OPEN WINDOW (BEN)

I was enjoying my music until my CD player got lifted. Damn, turned my back too long. I was over at Sisters of the Road Café playing some tunes, and this rager asked me if he could play his CD next. He'd come around once in a while and smoke you out. And he's pacing up and down to the beat and I said, "You really get into it, don't you?"

"Yeah," he said. "It relaxes me."

I didn't say anything, but I did wonder to myself what he looked like when he was nervous. I found out later he'd been going around raging for the lord all this time. A good reminder not to judge by the tats and the piercings. He wasn't the one who stole my CD player.

This is not meant to be some kind of inspirational tale. No one is going to try and tell you that when the lord closes one door he always opens another. What I am here to tell you is that when the lord closes all of your doors, he usually leaves a window open on one of the upper floors.

SURPRISE! (LAURA)

After a particularly wet and dispiriting spring (very few people wanted to stand outdoors talking about their favorite novel—everybody who could find shelter had done so), I received a phone call from a woman at the National Book Foundation. Street Books had won a prize! This meant $2,500 and a trip to New York, where I would be invited to speak at the Ford Foundation. In Portland, we'd had articles written about us in the *Oregonian*, the *Portland Mercury*, and the *Portland Tribune*. Suddenly, it felt like the little street library was starting to take off.

RANDOM KINDNESSES (BEN)

Now it's a naturopathic medical center; back then it was an abandoned building with a recessed doorway that I would sit in for hours at a stretch, out of the rain. Good hidey-hole. One day a guy walked past, I thought I recognized him from TPI back when I'd stayed there. A few seconds later, he reappeared, said, "Here, man," handed me a bill, and walked on. I looked at it, saw that it was a fifty, and sat there in stunned silence. I couldn't help but think of the Chinese penny I had picked up that morning.

That night I was awakened by a young woman from Newport who had just stepped out of a bar. She handed me a twenty-dollar bill. She wasn't used to seeing a lot of down-and-outers and generosity must have gotten the best of her. I looked at it and said, "Aw, you don't have to do that." She wasn't going to let me get away with that and handed me another one. The next morning, I took the penny out of my pocket and looked at it, thinking I don't really believe in lucky pennies, but if there's any luck in this one, I think I've just about milked it for all it's worth. I tossed it down for someone else to find. The only thing I was spending money on at the time was rolling tobacco, and that ninety dollars lasted me over three months. Sometime later, I ran into the guy who'd given me the fifty and asked him why he'd done it. He said he'd had a lot at the time, and I looked like I really needed help. Go figure that one out.

These small kindnesses I've spoken of: I've given them short shrift. I still haven't mentioned the outdoorsmen helping each other. Once when I was out canning, I encountered another guy that was doing the same, he gave me a bunch of cans. Bent over to pick up a half a cigarette and a guy said, "You want some snipes?" and gave me a tin with a bunch of half cigarettes.

Or the time I was bedding down for the night and the lady next to me had no further need for her paper shopping bag and asked me if I needed it. Considerate, no? Limited, perhaps, but there is such a thing as a sense of camaraderie in the outdoorsmen's community.

Funny how even if you don't know what to ask for, or how to ask if you did, the crowd in general might cover you. I was under the Steel Bridge once, trying to carve out a little space to set up, and the people that were already there sort of took me in. Someone pulled out a tarp for me. It was strange, even though I didn't really have the verbals, everybody sort of knew.

INVISIBLE MAN (LAURA)

It felt a little funny to be training Redd on how to be a street librarian, given that I'd just started doing it myself the summer before. I was no expert. But the ingredients were simple: bike to a spot, set the brake, pull out the drawer, and open the box. If we stopped in the same place, same time each week, the rest took care of itself: our regulars would return last week's books and check out new ones. The most important thing was remembering each person's name and doing one's best to fulfill their requests for the following week.

Redd worked for New Avenues for Youth and was studying to be a social worker. He was no stranger to working with people who had been pushed to the margins. I'd known him since the early nineties in Provo, when I'd been a student and we'd hung out at the same bookstore. I still recalled the terrifying motorcycle ride he took me on when I turned twenty-one, so I knew he had experience maneuvering a bike. I was grateful that fate had landed both of us in the same city and that he wanted to be a librarian for Street Books. Having a second librarian meant I could do more summer outings with my young family and not get worn down to such a nub as the previous summer.

His first shift started out quietly. There were more people stopping by to say, "What a great idea," than to check out a book. After Redd had taken the bike for a spin around the square, I noticed two men gliding around the periphery, glassy-eyed, their hands waving like undersea plants. They approached Redd where he had parked the bike, looked into the cart at the books, then glided back to the edges of the square. Other people gave them a wide berth to avoid an encounter. At one point, one of the men came close, knelt next to the shelf of books, and blew smoke along the length of it. Then he receded again, and a moment later came the foul smell of a rotten egg.

"Yuck," I said. "What was that?"

"Wow, that's meth he's smoking," Redd said. He had seen someone smoke it before and recognized the noxious smell.

Redd packed up the bike and took another slow circle around the square, getting the feel of the weight of it and practicing the foot brake. When one of the men approached him from behind and mimed a slow-motion stabbing gesture, we made our exit. That night I called him.

"Are you sure you still want to be a street librarian?" I asked.

"I am," he said.

Maybe it had been a good thing to have a vaguely creepy episode happen on the first day of the season, because it was a reminder that we needed to be alert. Weeks earlier in Florida, a man had gone on a drug-fueled attack in which he ate most of another man's face off. The police had shot him dead because he wouldn't stop. I knew I didn't want to expose myself to this kind of violence, no matter how committed I felt to bringing books to the people. But I also knew this: The man who'd been attacked had apparently been living outside, and by now I understood that people in his situation were more vulnerable than they were dangerous.

CANNING (BEN)

I had heard about it long before I ever started doing it. I'd be sitting on my park bench reading my book, and a guy I recognized from the shelter would stop by and talk. He told me that he got his tobacco money by walking around downtown checking the coin return slots on the parking meters. Most of them are empty, but if you check in two hundred of them, maybe as many as fifteen will have a little change in there. About eighteen months later, when I was at a winter shelter getting myself a little bit back together, I started doing it myself. It's not the kind of work experience you put on your résumé, but if the only thing you're spending money on is a little rolling tobacco, it's suitable for the task at hand.

One day I looked inside a recycling bin outside the Chinese food joint, and there were about fifty Red Bull cans in it, which I promptly bagged up and took over to Safeway for two and a half dollars. That was when I started pushing a shopping cart around with me. The first thing I learned is what a bother a shopping cart is. You have to walk around in front and pull and lift just to get it over the MAX tracks, and the curbs can be challenging as well. But it worked out, to a degree. I could find thirty-five cents in a meter and think *there's seven cans I don't have to pick up.* Or I could find fifteen cans in one spot and think *there's seventy-five cents I don't have to pull out of the meters.*

Downtown is a little thin in the canning department, but if your goal is only a buck or two, you can usually get it. I'd scrape meters from PSU downwards, and start canning a few blocks earlier than that. The canning enterprise soon outstripped the meter scraping, and as I expanded my route, the bottles were starting to weigh me down before I even got into town. Then I found a stroller in perfect working order, next to a dumpster, and suddenly the bottles were as weightless as the cans. A few dollars in the undercarriage, a duffel bag and a seabag full up top, a couple trash bags of cans tied on to the handlebar, and I was good to go. On a good day, I might hit Safeway right at eight when the recycling room opened with around $12.50 worth of returnables. On an off day it was still four bucks I didn't have yesterday, and I could go have lunch at Blanchet and then keep going. I started bopping over to the east side, finding little locations where the nickels were.

The canning game is screwy. There's the competition. Sometimes cans are all over, then there are times when you've hit fifteen spots and finally figure out that somebody has been there ahead of you. That's when you realize you've been outscrounged and move on. You switch over a few blocks, and then it's a thing of being in the right place at the right time. You find a sackful in a recycling bin, and some guy across the street comes out of his house with two more bags and asks you if you want them. That's a good day.

DISAPPEARING *T*'s (LAURA)

He had short curly dark hair with the beginning of light gray streaks. I'd run into him several times already, noting his homemade buttons, his zombie-fighting stickers and gear. He tended to disparage the people around him, citing their inferior intelligence and grubbiness and their lack of a place to stay (though I believe he was also living outdoors).

He asked if I remembered the host of the old *Twilight Zone* series.

"I think so," I said. "Wasn't it Rod Sterling?"

His eyes shone. "Exactly. Look at this." He produced a copy of *Twilight Zone* stories, published in 1960. On the cover it read *Rod Serling*. No *T*.

"How about Charlie Brown?" he said. "Who wrote Charlie Brown?"

"Charles Schul—" I began, but a patron spoke up first. "Schultz, spelled with a *T*, isn't it? S-c-h-u-l-t-z."

The zombie-hunter pulled out a classic *Peanuts* collection and showed us how the author's name was spelled Schulz, no *T*.

"So the *T*'s are missing from things?" I asked him.

"The *T*'s are disappearing, but it's not just that," he said. "We are undergoing a Satanic Lucification of things."

As near as I could tell, this had something to do with the guy who did fake sign language at Nelson Mandela's funeral, and how Mandela was rumored to have died in prison in the eighties. But the zombie-hunter's theory went further, involving several other celebrities who had died and then come back to life.

"How about the guy from *Charlie and the Chocolate Factory*?" he said.

"Gene Wilder?"

"Yeah, that guy. He's an example. Also, Muhammad Ali. He died and came back. Same with Karen Carpenter. They have pictures of her performing ten years after her death."

He cited other examples: Jiffy vs. Jif peanut butter. Febreze air freshener and how it had formerly had two *E*'s in breeze. The *E*'s were apparently disappearing as well.

I began to feel very tired. Beyond us, at the curb, a man in purple Converse sneakers and a tie-dyed shirt crooned into the bottom of his phone, which was playing a tinny "Ain't No Mountain High Enough." He was rocking out hard, oblivious to the people passing by with their work badges and takeout lunches, their shopping carts full of blankets and cardboard. Nothing slowed his dancing. I envied the world he inhabited, seemingly untroubled by Satan, zombies, or letters gone missing.

CANNING II (BEN)

The recycling bins are where you expect to find the returnables, but there are always those that do not adhere strictly to the guidelines, so the dumpsters are in play too, even though some folks don't like you going through there. And if the dumpster is nearly empty and you can't reach the bottom, but there happen to be a lot of cans in there just out of reach, you'll have to climb in, 'cause it's too many to leave behind.

One morning I was climbing back out of a dumpster just as a maintenance man was driving by on his golf cart, and he felt compelled to come over and tell me that I couldn't do that, that he was sorry, that he knows that it helps me, but that, "There's nothing I can do."

I didn't say anything. I just went on my way, thinking *how right you are, sir. There really isn't much you can do. I'll be back tomorrow, and the chances of you and I being here in the same five minutes are approximately nil.*

So you see why I didn't say anything. You really do need to be respectful. One complaint from a tenant and they would have to take sterner measures.

I learned to skulk about with all the stealth and secrecy of a ninja. I was at a different apartment building later on, and this place had a dumpster that was for cardboard. It had eight-foot walls on it so you couldn't just reach in. Somebody had put their cans in the wrong dumpster, and if it had been ten or fifteen cans I wouldn't have bothered, but there were so many in there it was like hitting the mother lode and I just could not leave all that behind. It was the dead of winter and everything was iced up. Just getting in and out of the thing without hurting myself was a master-work of planning and execution, and getting the full bags of cans out—silently—added a whole extra dimension to it. Just as I was climbing out, precariously balanced at the top, I heard someone say, "Okay, here's the deal." It was the man-ager, who had apparently caught my act before. "Don't make any noise," he said. "Don't go in the dumpsters too much. Don't hurt yourself." Fact is, there are liability issues, and he was probably supposed to tell me not to come back. It was a pleasing contrast to the "there's nothing I can do" at the other apartments.

When you're canning, mostly nobody gives a good god-damn what you're up to, and a few that are always ready to lend a hand. (I could be at the Plaid cashing in, and some stranger, seeing my plight, hands me three dollars.) I got the idea of taking the MAX out farther east and then working my way back in, rather than walking out and back. All be-cause of that stroller I saw parts of town I would never have otherwise seen, and I could bring things along that I would have left for lack of cargo space. Good stuff, too. Few there be who have a stuffed armadillo, and I had to be the only outdoorsman that had one. Not a toy, a real armadillo. I called him Armando. Good company, too, never gave me no backsass. Armandistas. I like to imagine a whole pack of renegade armadillos running a street gang down in Texas.

TRUE CRIME (LAURA)

It was the middle of summer, 2012. Second season of Street Books and a sense that anything was possible. It was Redd, Beth, and me, and we were building it into something real. I was more confident this second season. People were always waiting for me when I pulled up on the bike and opened up the library. I trusted the conversations and the people. Then I read about Niki Powell. She was in her early thirties, a faithful volunteer three nights a week at Operation Nightwatch, an ecumenical ministry that opened up in the evenings for people to have a coffee, play cards, and be a part of a community. She had apparently given an extra set of her apartment keys to a man she'd met at Operation Nightwatch, to help him get through a rough patch. And instead of returning her gesture with kindness, he'd assaulted her, strangled her with a shoelace, and left her in her bed, where she was discovered a week later. She hadn't known the man was a registered sex offender. I was so chilled when I read about this in the *Oregonian* that my heart froze.

I thought of Niki Powell's family and I thought of my little daughter and I thought about whether or not I was taking an enormous risk every time I ventured onto the street to work the street library. I thought about Niki Powell every day for the rest of that summer, calling up the smiling pictures I'd seen of her in the newspaper and the kind of good she'd been trying to do in the world. I considered my own carefully constructed edifice of security, based on a year of positive experiences with my Street Books patrons, and the way I used this as a shield or a talisman each time I ventured out on the bicycle. I knew that I needed to be careful. But I didn't want to be afraid.

INNOCENCE (BEN)

Alexander Pope once wrote, "He's armed without that's innocent within."

I don't know if that's true or not. Judge for yourself. You could just as easily say, "He's a sitting duck that's naive." But there was this one guy. The most unlikely guy you ever saw out here.

It was like looking at a picture and being asked, "What's wrong with this picture?"

And you looked and said, "It's that guy right there. That guy doesn't belong in this picture."

That was Joseph.

I had seen him around several times, and later, when we were both in the same shelter, I got the story.

His mom was in New Orleans, his dad was in Alaska, he'd done some traveling.

He was a ballet dancer.

No wonder he didn't fit in the picture.

A complete innocent in a world of cutthroats and vipers.

When he came into the shelter, nobody told him that you get UA'd after a week.

And when somebody offered him some puffs, he graciously assented.

And when he came up positive, they sent him over to the parole officer types.

Who informed him what a piece of shit he was.

That if he don't change his ways he's not gonna believe what happens next.

And he was baffled.

He couldn't understand why people were saying mean words to him.

He had gotten shot in the head.

In New Orleans. He was riding his bike and all he remembered was coming off his bike and when he woke up in the hospital his mom told him he'd gotten shot.

Sometimes a bullet can go through the brain and you'd never know there was anything wrong with the guy, and if Joe was missing anything, he wasn't missing much.

What he had was that protective bubble of innocence.

Talk about someone who just plain didn't belong here.

His resources dwindled; his van got towed.

Someone who may or may not have been his cousin moved him into his house out on Capitol Highway.

Just because of his outlook, there was only a minimal amount of evil that could congeal on him.

The last time I talked to him it was on the phone, and he was in North Carolina, at some furniture-moving deal. If he ever makes it back on the stage, I want to see it.

WHAT WE CARRY (LAURA)

I recognized her voice before I remembered the rest of her. But I wasn't sure. She inspected the books on the Street Books shelf, and we talked about reading. She loved to read. She shot me a look.

"Do I know you from someplace?"

"Have you checked out books with us before?"

She shook her head slowly. "No, that wouldn't be it."

Now I was almost sure. "Have you ever lived in Wilsonville?"

"No," she said. "I drove cab, but never that far out of town."

We went back and forth this way, until it was almost funny.

"Oh," she said. "I served nineteen years out at Coffee Creek for armed robbery and murder."

"You were in my writing class," I said.

"That's right! I remember now."

In the workshop at the prison, we had written about the jobs we'd had. We'd written about objects that were precious to us, memories from childhood. We'd read poetry by Pablo Neruda and Dorianne Laux. I had been pregnant with Coen when I taught the workshop, and the women offered unsolicited advice on how to give birth. Suggestions like, "Just eat a bag of those little Hershey's chocolates when you start feeling the pains come on. And it helps if you have a bar to hang from and a towel to chew on." They'd laughed at the expression on my face, and then debated what the pain was like. Deb said it was no worse than a big bowel movement.

"That's bullshit," Tanika said. "It's a *train wreck* through your privates."

I looked at Carol standing next to me at the bike library all these years later. My son was seven now.

"You are a great writer," I told her. And she was. She'd written about her life, her ambitions, and the time she'd gone into a convenience store, high on drugs, with a gun she'd borrowed from an acquaintance. She'd written about the clerk she'd shot during the robbery, and how her children had grown up without their mother. She'd also written about her own children, and how they had lived nearly two decades without a mother.

I remembered her neat script and how she composed in cursive.

"I gotta stay light on my feet out here," she said, so she didn't check out a book.

DAVIS STREET
BEAUTIFICATION PROJECT (BEN)

It's not how many times you fall down, it's how many times you get back up. Or, it's falling down so many times that eventually you land in a comfortable spot.

One of the happiest periods of my street life was when I cleaned up Davis Street between Third and Fourth, where there were four planter boxes with a palm tree and a shrub or rose bush in each. The debris had accumulated over who knows how long. I dumpster-dived a push broom and started cleaning around the planter nearest the Chinese food joint where I was sleeping at the time. Not long after I'd started spiffing up the block, I saw a billboard announcing that the Dalai Lama was coming to town. That was what really kicked it into high gear. On the off chance that he decided to swing through Chinatown while he was here, we needed to get the place looking right. I mean all the way down to scraping the dirt out of the cracks in the sidewalk. I had a length of hose and a five-gallon bucket, and there was a bathroom down at the parking garage where I stopped up the sink and siphoned hot water into my bucket, hung it on the handlebar of my bike, and walked it three blocks back to the job site.

This was a good start, but what to do about a Tibetan flag? At a Chinese-owned travel agency right on that very block, I went in and explained to the woman working there about His Holiness coming and asked if they had a picture of the flag, but no luck. Then I asked if she knew anyone who spoke Tibetan.

"No," she said. "Why?" I told her I wanted to learn how to say, "You got any spare change?" in Tibetan. She almost didn't smile and said, "Shame on you."

The poster shop at Lloyd Center did have a small 3x5 Tibetan flag, and the clerk gave me a postcard with the Dalai Lama's picture on it. You know how one thing sometimes leads to another? I told someone about it, and then someone else's mom had a full-size Tibetan flag, and we had a good head of steam going back on Davis Street. There were a few enlistees that joined up. Lucky only stuck around for about forty-five minutes, but forty-five minutes of Lucky is a lot; as a former logger, he knows what work is. His friend Toby also pitched in. Chudznik, the Polish guy from Caracas, was willing, but I'm afraid he turned out to be a bit of a hobble-dehoy.

A lot of crud builds up over time: dead grass, cigarette butts, old needles, scraps of paper. There was at least one big trash bag per planter box. As I scrubbed the bronze plaques set into the sidewalk, and scraped the gum off, I thought, *here is something I can do without getting hassled.* But I was wrong. One guy came by and suggested I try AA. I also got some flak for the pruning of the palm trees. It was a bit of a struggle doing it with just a pair of a scissors, but it worked, sort of. A couple of gentlemen from Clean & Safe told me that there were people from the city that took care of that, so I should cease and desist. I didn't bother asking them where the city people had been for the past few years. I just focused on something else until they left and then got back to work. Later, a friendly guy from Clean & Safe came by and said he'd watched me trying to make the scissors work. He loaned me a pair of pruners and said if he didn't get them back, then he should have used better judgment (he got the pruners back).

Two of the local merchants stopped by with drinks: a Dr Pepper and an orange juice. The director of the Chinese Garden stopped once and told me she'd noticed it gradually looking better over the weeks.

There were three of us working on it the same day as some roadwork on Third was going on. "I've been here for over an hour watching you people going at it with everything but a toothbrush," the flagger said to us.

"Oh, you mean this toothbrush?" I said, holding it aloft.

THE WORKER CENTER (LAURA)

The men were from Mexico mostly, but once in a while I met someone from Central or South America. When I started the library shift at the Worker Center, I dusted off the Spanish I'd learned while living in Ecuador for six months in 2002. Though I'd gotten some practice with the parents from Rigler Elementary since then, I knew my Spanish wasn't at a level that would allow me to have a conversation about books. But the library patrons at the Worker Center were very patient with me. They were glad to see the books, and nobody seemed to mind if I couldn't go very deep about literature.

The schedule was the same each week. Men gathered to get their names on a list, in hopes that people would come in search of laborers for painting, yardwork, and so on. At noon, Andreas honked and pulled his food truck into the parking lot. We knew each other because he also had kids at Rigler and often offered me a free taco. Alongside Andreas, the regular cast of characters in the lot included Douglas, a volunteer photographer, and John, a wage theft volunteer who stuck around to make sure the workers got paid.

Everyone liked the dream interpretation manual, el *Diccionario de los sueños*. It became a running joke, and most every week one of the guys would approach with a dream and we'd look it up to see what it meant. Juan told me he'd dreamt of rocks floating around his head and torso—not alarming but very surreal. The nearest thing to *Rocks* we could find in the book was *Comets*.

Juan shrugged. "Maybe they were a bit like comets," he said.

According to the manual, dreaming of a comet was an auspicious sign because any kind of meteor or star crossing the sky in a dream meant something good on its way, potential energy in the making.

ART (BEN)

I found a book of impressionist art in a free box on Powell Street. Genet's *Querelle of Brest*, Antonin Artaud's *Heliogabulus*. Not a bad score for just walking around. So once I was done cleaning the block, I decided to spruce up the space outside the Chinese food joint, which had been closed-up for some years by then. A Renoir here, a Degas just there. I cut out thirteen or so pieces, paintings like *L'Absinthe* and *At the Moulin Rouge*, and using duct tape to simulate frames, put up a real nice display on the windows. The duct tape looked real sharp, and being so firmly fixed in place, I figured the art would probably stay up there a good long time. I kept running out of duct tape and could only afford a small roll at a time, so it took a little over a week to fill up the available window and door space with thirteen priceless masterpieces. I wondered how many millions it would add up to if those had been the originals.

You need to be timely about clearing yourself and your stuff off the street in the morning, and I forget now why I left or what the delay was getting back, but one day I hustled back a little too late, and wouldn't you know it, Clean & Safe had made off with my cleaning stuff, bucket and all. It threw me for a bit, but then I said to myself, only slightly daunted, "I did not get where I am today by giving up so easy." Some clear, quick thinking was in order. What I did was, under the guise of cleaning up around *Street Roots* (for extra newspapers to sell), I spirited a few cleaning supplies out, and in less than a week I was back on the job.

Tourists were stopping and taking pictures of it, that's how good it looked, but you know, nothing lasts forever, especially with Clean & Safe on the job. Two weeks later I got back one Friday evening and it was all gone. Well, not quite all of it. The beautiful pictures were gone, but a lot of the ugly looking duct tape frames were still there.

LECTURE (LAURA)

As part of the class I was teaching as an adjunct professor at Lewis & Clark, my students and I took a walking fieldtrip to the R2D2 rest area at Fourth and Burnside. I'd arranged a meeting with a resident there named Dikweed (spelled without the *C*, he explained, so as not to offend anyone). A giant man with a shaved head and beard, he had a professorial bearing and a droll sense of humor. His talk incorporated precepts of Buddhism while he described the monastic life he led at the camp. I could tell it made an impression on my students. I waved down a *Street Roots* vendor in the background and he came over and sold some newspapers when Dikweed was done.

A NAP INDOORS (BEN)

One day, my friend Dawn and I stopped in to visit her friend Debbie at the Martha Washington. It's one of those places with a visitor's log, and the host has to let you in. I wouldn't want to live in a place like that. This was the first time I had been inside a residence in over two years, and it was weird. What happens is, you been outside for so long that you do not notice how hard you are pushing yourself. And the second I walked through the doorway a huge wave of exhaustion hit me real hard, just exactly the way a huge wave of something would hit you, and I walked across the room and flopped down on the floor and slept solid for a couple hours. Then I got the shower that had been offered, and actually felt like a million bucks for a short time there. We hung out for another couple of hours while Debbie hustled up something to eat, and talked, and talked, and talked some more. Then later, she talked about things. I'm pretty sure she was still talking when we left. I mentioned later to someone else who knew her about how much Debbie talked, and was given reassurances that I had not seen anything yet.

TEACHING (LAURA)

At Marylhurst University, I taught a creative nonfiction class I called "Writing & Service: Documenting Lives in the City." Students visited the street library to get an idea of what happened there. They were asked to do observational writing in the city. The final project was to find and document a story that would otherwise go untold. This was something I'd been trying to do all along with Street Books, document the conversations I was having and capture stories from people willing to share them. My students' work impressed me. Rick, an Iraq and Afghanistan veteran, sought out an Afghan man who worked at a convenience store in his neighborhood. He interviewed him and discovered that they'd lived in the same places. Jeffrey knew well what it was like to live outside, and so he focused on someone inside: a friend who had come close to taking his own life who had worked his way back into health. Suzanne, a student in her midfifties who was quite shy, had screwed up her courage to approach a man who she'd noticed sitting in a wheelchair in a park, his backpack next to him on the ground. He'd filled her ear (and her notebook) with the stories of his life, and she was radiant the night she presented her findings in class. I loved watching students take a risk and talk to someone they didn't know.

TRY HILLSBORO (BEN)

Somewhere up around NE Schuyler or Thompson at about Eighth there's an alley that's a good place to lurk. I was lurking, breaking apart a six-pack and stowing the cans in my pack, when the black-and-white rolled past, then stopped, backed up, and rolled up the alley. Had I stood up and showed them that none of the beer was being consumed, only transferred, their reason for checking me out would have gone and they would have gone. Instead I offered up my ID as asked.

Now, here is a lesson that every grade school kid should know. When the police say, "You don't have warrants, do you?" you are supposed to say, "Oh, no, nothing like that." But I did not say that to the officer. What I told her was, "Try Hillsboro." I had missed a court date and thought it might be time to get to the bottom of the situation. So, she did try Hillsboro and they did have a warrant out for me. Resistance was useless. I even asked her, "You're not going to take me in, are you?" She was going to, and "I have to" was the reason. Even though she knew by now that there never was an open container, and even though the original inquiry was perhaps unjustified, the information obtained was compelling.

And so I was compelled to take a car ride downtown, but I didn't feel too bad about it. We pulled up in front of the place, and she stopped to fill out the last of the paperwork.

Our time together was coming to a close, and I didn't quite know how to broach the subject.

So I just said, "I hope you don't mind my saying so, but for a blind date, this has been a lot more fun than I expected." She looked at me in the mirror a bit, then we drove inside.

END OF SEASON TWO (LAURA)

At the end of the second season, we held a reception at Bud Clark Commons, a space inside the day center with apartments serving people coming off the streets. Even though I had been feeling more confident running the library, it didn't mean I was good at hosting events. We'd gotten items donated for an auction so we could assemble themed baskets featuring wine, books, or knee socks. But I flubbed up and wrote in the actual value of each basket as the starting bid, which put the baskets financially out of reach for all of our patrons along with most of our supporters, many of whom were writers and artists. I also hadn't reckoned on the number of folks at Bud Clark who were happy to file in for a free meal, even if they'd never checked out a book from Street Books. Would we have enough food? I decided it didn't matter and I invited everyone inside. I hadn't thought to arrange to have a microphone, but our guest speaker, Mark Hubble, who was still a resident of R2D2, projected the best he could. He spoke about meeting the writer Ray Bradbury when he was young, and how important that had been to his life. He talked about the books he'd checked out from the Street Books library and his gratitude for the community.

Diana, the scrappy winner of the women's division at the Disaster Relief Trials cargo bike race that year, showed up with her cargo bike full of drinks for the reception. After the reception, it was like a switch had been flipped. A whole crew of folks were willing to give their time and talents to the street library: Tracy, the accountant, would join the board; and Rachel, who lived in her car with Sebastian the dog, would become a street librarian. Austin, friend of Redd, would become a street librarian–turned–office manager. Native Spanish speakers Pépe, Pati, and Marissa would deepen conversations at the Worker Center library shifts. Retired school librarian Betsy would later read about Street Books in the *Oregonian* and join our board. Olive, whose encyclopedic knowledge of everything, mixed with her attentive bedside manner at library shifts, would fast become a favorite with patrons. Byrd and Pati, both legit librarians from Multnomah County, would join the board. Writer and retired educator Robin would join the board and eventually take over as board president. Merüch, who lived out of his van, and Nika, whom we met at p:ear, would both join the team as street librarians. Sofie would come on as a librarian and go on to help with social media and operating new library shifts indoors. The fall of 2012 was when Street Books really started to feel like a family.

SURVEILLANCE (BEN)

TPI was vastly improved from their old location, but I did not like the sign posted on the pillar in the common room. ARE YOU TEACHABLE? they wanted to know. What an insult. The obvious implication is that no, of course we are not and that's why we're here. It's the damn parole board mentality that permeates the place. I didn't object to the surveillance cameras in the sleeping area. If someone was going into a locker that wasn't theirs, they'd get caught. It was the one in the courtyard that bothered me.

UNWELCOME (LAURA)

JJ came early to give me a hand at our Atrium Gallery event in Old Town. He stashed his giant army rucksack in the foyer and hustled around helping me set up tables and chairs. Then he took a break, and was putting something into his rucksack or taking something out—whatever, it doesn't matter—the point is that one of the guys who owned the gallery, or maybe it was the building owner, stopped up short in the foyer and said, "Can I help you with something?" but it wasn't the friendly kind of *can I help you?* It was the version that means *you should not be here.*

And I had to say, "He's with me, he's helping to set up for an event," and the guy eased up. But it reminded me of how I'm privileged, how I look vaguely showered and spruced up, which apparently allows me to speak for those whose personal hygiene opportunities are few and far between. And that's messed up.

SHOUTING BACK (BEN)

Everybody's had dreams that are impossible. Like you're flying or at the bottom of the ocean talking to people. Or in my case: I'm on the third floor of a building under construction, only the whole thing is made out of tongue depressors. Obviously quite impossible, but it didn't bother me.

I made my way across a beam, and some guy from down below shouts up at me in a rude fashion, "What the hell do you think . . . ," something of that order.

Sticking up for myself has really never been my strong suit. And since I'd been outdoors for two years, unable to even speak to anybody, sticking up for myself was just about out of the question. But in the dream, I got right back in his face, basically you could fit a lot of curse words into what I said to him.

Look at the symbolism here. Is it really possible this is a specious connection, or does it make perfect sense? Tongue depressors? Unable to speak? Do we see a connection? Well, could be a bit sketchy, but make of it what you will. (Don't think I don't know that my dream analysis is probably the worst butchering of Jung and Freud you've ever seen, but it's still true that it was around this time that I started to come back to life. I decided to face up to the hassles with my leg and do whatever it took to get off the books.)

The dream faded out, and the rest is forgotten, but the point is—in the dream I stuck up for myself, and the very next day, and for the first time in two years, I began trying to take care of myself. To take stock of the whole situation and meet everything head-on. It's like Mose Allison says, "When you get up to the city, you better learn to shout. Cause if you don't stand up and holler, you're gonna get left out."

That was the time when I took ten dollars out of the last little bit of money I had, put it in a cigarette pack, and put the cigarette pack behind this pole where there was a spot I could hide it, partially concealed by a bush. Nobody was gonna find it. This way when I got out of jail, I wouldn't be completely broke. So I went all the way out to Hillsboro.

"Here I am, fellas," I said.

"What, you got a warrant or something? Let's see some ID?"

"Yes sir, a known miscreant," I told them, and they let me in.

I think I was in there for twenty days. It was at least ten, but I think it was twenty. And when I got out, sure enough, there was my ten bucks in the cigarette pack. That was when I started to turn everything around.

THE ANSWER (LAURA)

Students from the Art and Social Practice program at PSU took over a vacant storefront and used the space for meetings and meals and artist talks. They invited me to set up the bike library in the window. This was good timing because I was no longer storing it at the Mercy Corps Action Center—that had ended with the first season—and I was relieved that I'd have a place for it to live. They helped me set it up on a platform, level with the window. I arranged books around it and hung a sign: STREET BOOKS IS A BICYCLE-POWERED MOBILE LIBRARY SERVING PEOPLE WHO LIVE OUTSIDE. They gave me a key and I left feeling very official and grateful.

But when I returned the following week, I was confronted by a dilemma: I was alone this time, and there was no way I could get the bike down from the platform, even when it was empty. It was just too heavy and impossible to lower off the platform by myself. I felt terrible, thinking of the patrons who would be waiting in the Park Blocks and near Skidmore Fountain. I kept an eye on the people passing by, searching for someone who looked both friendly and sturdy enough to hoist the bike. I leaned against the window and felt the courage drain from me—maybe I wasn't up for rallying somebody to help me after all. But then, all of a sudden, as though the clouds were parting and letting the sunshine through, here came Mattias from the previous summer. Mattias, friendly and deferential, barely twenty and recently housed after a stint of living outdoors. Mattias, who was studying organic gardening so he could start his own farm someday. Mattias, who had requested the raw foods book and then disappeared the next week when we had a copy for him.

Would he help me? As it happened, yes, he was glad to. And even though he knew it was a long shot, after all this time, did we still have a copy of that book on raw foods? Also yes. These were the kinds of Street Books miracles I lived for.

NEXT STEPS (BEN)

To make it off the streets you have to have a working cell phone, web access, a clean record, a valid ID, and, dare I speak the unspeakable word, a [JOB]. A car doesn't hurt, a bank account, a credit number that's bigger than one, and some jingle in your pocket. Wait a minute, don't forget clean clothes and an occasional haircut. This is the quantum leap concept, how if you don't have all of it, you don't have any of it. Then it takes ninety days to find an apartment. Small wonder some guys just prefer to fly off the radar.

NOTE TO SELF (LAURA)

Joseph Beuys did some kind of project in which he lived in a gallery with a coyote. I think it was controversial (I'm guessing the coyote didn't sign a consent form to participate). The two circled around each other with great wariness. That's how I'm feeling today as I sit down to write, a wary circling around myself. What will I do with this time? After allowing myself to be pulled thin in many directions, what can I make when left to my own devices? (Let's face it: Some of this is my own doing—I sign up for too much. *Here lies Laura, she signed up for too much.*) Both kids are at the elementary school now, which offers an incredible stretch of uninterrupted hours. I need to sketch out my initial plan: First, create a sketch of what a Street Books book could look like. So for now, my plan is to write like crazy about Street Books, try to capture the quality of a Street Books library shift while it's fresh in my mind.

A RED-LETTER DAY (BEN)

You had to be standing in the right spot to see it, which is why it stayed there all night. It was a full pack of cigarettes, in the gutter between a car tire and the curb. I was standing in the right spot, watering the flowers close to the curb, and first thing in the morning I had myself a whole pack of smokes. Not much later, me and Lucky were walking under the Burnside Bridge, and he reached into the ticket machine at the MAX stop and pulled out two all-day passes and some change, which was very lucky, because you never find anything in those machines.

Not ten minutes later, we passed a dumpster at a construction job, and there were three large bags full of cans in there. Since we had the bus passes, we decided to take them up to the Burlingame Fred Meyer, where they don't care if you go over the limit. While we were running them through the recycling machine, somebody came by with a couple full bags of cans, saw how crowded it was, decided that their time was worth more than the money, and asked if we wanted their cans. Now we were about thirty-five dollars to the good, if you counted the cigarettes and the bus passes.

On the ride back, I asked Lucky if he had seen that footpath that ran up through the woods that we'd passed on the way there. "Yeah, I did see that," he said. "You think we should try it?" So we decided to do a little exploring and see what we could see. We headed up the path and came to a little side path leading up to the right. Not much farther up, we came across an abandoned campsite, mostly a whole lot of trash, but some usable stuff too—a few tarps and about a hundred feet of some really good rope.

At first, we were just killing time and having a drink, but looking around, I started to get big ideas about the possibilities in this place, so I started bagging up the trash.

CEREMONY (LAURA)

Merüch lived out of a battered van and I only knew a few things about him: He was from Colorado and had been a regular last summer at our Sisters of the Road shift. Rachel and Austin had recommended him after he mentioned he was interested in working for Street Books.

The job interview took place on the corner of NW Sixth and Davis, next to the bike library. He told me that one of his favorite books was *Ceremony*, by Leslie Marmon Silko, and that the street librarians had found him a copy after he'd lost his years before. We gave him one of our blue Street Books T-shirts. He would work at the Trinity shift as an assistant to Diana, who had become a beloved street librarian by then.

One day, Merüch visited Pépe and me on the shift at St. Francis. While we were standing there talking, a man approached. He was tan, with bright-blue eyes and a Prince Valiant pageboy haircut. He had kind of a surfer vibe, bouncing on the balls of his feet as he spoke.

"Sorry to interrupt," he said, extending his fist so that we each tentatively bumped it. "I've been working on my cuticles. You know how they can be either diastolic or systolic? You know how one means that you're healthy and one means your body is consuming itself?"

We didn't know that, as it happened. But the man didn't wait for our answer.

"Well, I've been scrubbing and scrubbing mine." He extended his fingers to show us his cuticles, and we leaned in politely to have a look. Then he moved away from us, still light on his feet.

"Hey, heads-up," I said and extended my hand, but he was already stepping backward into the heavy concrete cylinder that held the garbage can. It took him by surprise, and he sprang forward and struck out with his fist, hitting Merüch on the shoulder.

"What the fuck," said a nearby library patron. "Back off, man." There was a low murmur from other patrons as well. They gathered around us to see what might be required of them. We had some very loyal patrons who didn't tolerate abuse of the librarians.

The man continued his wired, nervous dance down the sidewalk, turning back and speaking to Merüch.

"She was trying to tell me something and I didn't see it and I . . . do you forgive me? I'm sorry. Do you forgive me?"

Merüch said, "Yes, yes, don't worry. I forgive you."

The man with the very clean cuticles dance-stepped his nervous jitterbug away, and we stood in the space his absence left. Somehow Merüch had kept his cool, even when he'd been struck. Even though he had a bandage on his forehead covering a wound he'd gotten just last week when he'd been jumped by some younger punks.

CAMPSITE (BEN)

"It was the clear morning I had waited for, as I had resolved to explore the land further up to see what provisions might be had there. So having breakfasted, I took up a musket, a brace of pistols and my fowling piece, and set off up the hill."

Well, I didn't actually have a brace of pistols like Robinson Crusoe, but I did spread out the rope and tarp I had stored away and started setting up. I threaded the rope through the eyelets in the tarps, tied it all off on the trees, sloping it artfully so that the rain would drip off on the downhill side. Just like that, I had a really nice little shelter. The previous occupants had used a dead pine tree set on a rise to block the site from view of the pathway. I went one better. I lashed some fallen branches to the trees, making a latticework, weaving some ivy through it to make a natural-looking wall that would conceal the site. Not exactly invisible, but unobtrusive enough to at least make it look like I'd made an effort.

My first chair was an overturned bucket. So was the second one, which meant the first one could be downgraded to a wastebasket. I'd be out and around, and I'd find things and lug them up to the campsite. Somebody brought up some hand sanitizer and a tin can and showed me how to make a small cooking fire. Worked just like a can of Sterno. I put some filler down in the bottom of the can, crumpled up newspaper, and found something that worked as a wick. The alcohol in the hand sanitizer made a nice blaze, suitable for cooking. One tip: it evaporates if you don't keep it covered, so my venture into that system didn't last long—I'd already moved up to a propane burner before the last of the hand sanitizer ran out. Picked it up at the Walmart on 82nd for a real good price. They may as well be giving them away at those prices. Makes you wonder how they stay in business. The folding canvas chair came next, followed by the aluminum folding chair. Soon, the place started to resemble a fairly well-appointed studio apartment.

Having a place to keep my stuff and not have to carry it all around with me, that was one of those quantum leaps. It's not realistic to even try to go out canning if you're already weighted down. Anything particularly valuable that I was worried about, I could tuck back in the ring of the seven trees, or any other hiding place, so that even if my campsite did get raided, I'd still have that.

Right from the get there was an aura of intrigue and romance about the place. It was the bent wire art that did it, fifty or more pieces of it scattered about. Mostly bent into the shapes of names. A friend told me that he remembered seeing the guy selling the stuff at the Saturday Market. I found wire that spelled "Yuric" and "Yurica," and wondered if that was their names, the ones who had camped there before me. After all, how could the Saturday Market guy have expected to sell a Yuric and a Yurica in Portland?

I particularly liked the diminutive piece that said "smaller." That must have been when he was teaching himself to make the letters smaller. I still have that one.

HEROES (LAURA)

On a trip to the Gorge, I met Tom, who runs Artifacts in Hood River, a cool bookstore selling new and used books along with fake mustaches, homemade duct tape wallets, etc. When I told him I operated Street Books in Portland, he wouldn't let me pay for the stack of anthologies I'd brought in from the shelves on the sidewalk, and in fact gave me a zine called *Cometbus* by a guy named Aaron Cometbus, who was something of a legend in the zinester world and now owned a bookstore in Brooklyn.

"You're one of our heroes," Tom said.

I didn't know what to say. It didn't feel particularly heroic to be showing up on the streets with books. I thought that if anybody was heroic, it was the person who'd been sleeping on cardboard on the sidewalk for months and yet still managed to stand up, shake off the stiffness, and come talk to me about Faulkner. But Tom's words made me feel good.

Back in Portland, I read Cometbus, absorbing his straightforward narrative about his Ukrainian friend Yula, how they sat on the same newspaper box each day, whiling away their time in Berkeley, feeling antiestablishment and loose at the joints, curious about a communist newspaper that was published sporadically. I also read his manifesto about zinemaking, publishing, and supporting one another's art—all of it was good for me to read, and a reminder that the giant [STORY] of Street Books I'd constructed in my mind, one that had a certain publishing house and a fancy cover—all of that big thinking might have stalled me out. Maybe it's as simple as this: You just tell the story in your own voice and try to write down as many details as you can remember. You don't fret about the possibility that by including snapshots of someone else's life you are appropriating their experiences as your own. You don't quote James Agee in a vague, unsupportable way, how he too worried about his role in telling the stories of the sharecroppers he interviewed in *Let Us Now Praise Famous Men*. You just write it down the best you can.

CAMPSITE II (BEN)

It was having a cup of coffee every morning, more than anything else, that made me feel like a human being. I did a little cooking for a while, but that eventually became too much of a bother, and peanut butter sandwiches became a big feature of my diet. I was conscientious about packing out the garbage from the campsite. Trash bags, slightly used, are readily available at the can return area at the supermarkets. I had found a little Styrofoam cooler to keep the milk drinkable, and that was what triggered the war with the rats.

I never did read *Walden*, but I bet even Thoreau would have been as torqued with the rats as I was. I suppose the strange thing is that it took them so long to launch the invasion. I'd had the cooler a good two or three weeks before I came back one day and saw the hole gnawed in it. It was the smell of the bread that drew them. I sensed that I was in a losing battle, but I had to push back. I slapped a few layers of duct tape over the hole. They worked around it. I sliced an aluminum can into a flat piece and taped that over the hole. They worked around it. I hung the bread from a tree branch and they crawled down the rope and got into it. They prevailed in the end, and I could no longer keep a loaf of bread at the campsite without having it violated, so I had to give up on my peanut butter sandwiches and switch to something else. One day at a MAX stop by the waterfront, some tourists who'd had too much to carry asked me if I wanted a cooler, a good solid plastic one. Ratproof, thank you very much. I still tossed the rats a few slices once in a while, to show no hard feelings. I didn't see why I had to sink to their level, the little rats.

SWEEPS <small>(LAURA)</small>

The mayor of Portland ordered the police to conduct sweeps on sidewalks and under bridges, moving people along who had set up tents or makeshift cardboard shelters. In Fresno, California, police performed similar sweeps and razed encampments. In Columbia, South Carolina, the city council banned people experiencing houselessness from being in the downtown area: Their options were jail or a shelter at the edge of town. Similar stories were coming from cities across the country. The police, I suspect, were looking for the same things as I had on that first day out delivering books on the bike: human beings reduced by their circumstances. The evidence? A backpack, a bedroll, a folded tarp tucked under one arm, and no particular place to go.

VISITOR (BEN)

I don't remember how it is I got to know Nicole, but she came up to the campsite once. I didn't notice anything amiss until after we got up there. She had some foil over her eyes, to keep out the signals, she said. I gave her time to get her bearings, and then got her back to town and places she knew. She'd always been conversational before, and it must have been one of those a-little-too-long-off-the-meds things. I hadn't even known she was on meds. For some reason it made me dislike her old boyfriend even more, but he probably hadn't known any more about it than I did. Most likely he wasn't taking advantage of her, but was just too dumb to notice that he wasn't doing her much good. You have to know not to judge people, and if some folks make you work harder at it than others, the point is still the same.

WHOLE GRAIN (LAURA)

The addition of librarians Pépe, Marissa, and Pati to the Worker Center took the pressure off my novice Spanish, and I loved the exchanges I got to hear and partially understand. Conversations about books and about the politics of the day.

The guys requested dictionaries, easy readers, graphic novels, comics. Alejandro was reading Carl Jung in English but wanted to get it in Spanish. I wrote down his request: *El hombre y sus símbolos.* I brought books by Gabriel García Márquez, Mario Vargas Llosa, Carlos Fuentes. Galeano's *Las venas abiertas de América Latina* and *Cajas de Cartón* by Francisco Jiménez.

I brought a bible for César—the week before, he'd requested *Designio*. We looked it up on my phone and it means "The Plan." But he looked at the bible I offered and shook his head. It wasn't what he'd meant. The word at the Center was that César had witnessed terrible things during a war in his country, but it wasn't something I felt comfortable asking him about. He often sat in the lot and fed bread to the pigeons.

Juan was a poet and a very regular patron at the library. He gestured to César and the pigeons and said he didn't approve of white bread going to the birds.

"That can't be good for their bodies," he said. "Something whole grain would be better." Juan was a vegan who lived in a shed. No electricity or plumbing but he said he got by just fine.

Martín told Pati and me, "En esta vida, hay que probar las dulces y las amargas." In this life, one must taste the sweet with the bitter. It was an apt description of the average Street Books library shift: Up close against the saddest and loveliest things at once, there was most always something bittersweet.

BACK TO SCHOOL (BEN)

It had seemed like a good idea at the time. The VA rep at Central City Concern put me on to a vocational rehab program that offered a stipend to go back to school, a sort of second chance GI bill. A refresher course or two and I'd look much better in the job market. Op Amp Circuits was the heavy class, but it was the other ones that weighed me down. Even then I'd still have made it through but for some legal difficulties, which caused me to miss a midterm, and then later, my pack with all my notebooks got lifted off the street.

That was about when I gave up on the school idea and switched to cleaning up Davis Street. I spent the whole next semester moving up to my new home in the hills, and it wasn't until the summer session that I got the idea of trying it again.

As I said, it seemed like a good idea at the time. I signed up for another twelve units and made another go of it. It didn't quite work out this time either, but it took a long time to unravel. The housing authority finally put me on the waiting list, and it looked like I was going to make it inside a lot faster than I would have if I had been left to my own devices. I'd rather have done it by being self-sufficient, but I wasn't in a position to be picky. As soon as they told me that I would be getting an apartment in six months I felt a lot better.

That was when I saw Laura again.

HAPPY ENDING (LAURA)

Every year I told myself it was better not to bump into any of my former patrons. Not seeing them meant there was a chance they'd managed to secure housing or experienced some change of fortune. I still looked for my favorites, though, and that week when I looked up from my shift in Chinatown, tears sprang to my eyes. There was Ben Hodgson, whom I hadn't seen since the afternoon two years earlier when he'd checked out Orwell. I grabbed him in a hug before he could speak, and when we stepped back from each other, he laughed, pleased. He looked more collected than I remembered, healthy. He told me that he had managed to mostly ditch the depression plaguing him when we'd first encountered each other two years earlier, and that even though he was still outside, he had a safe place to camp and plenty to eat.

"Do you want to go have a coffee," I said, "and you can tell me your adventures since I saw you last?"

HAPPY ENDING II (BEN)

I stumbled across Laura at tent city, with the bike. She looked radiant. She reached out her hand, took a step toward me, then got her feet set and dropped a vicious right cross on my jaw, saying, "Where the hell you been, asshat?" I didn't know what to say, and couldn't have said it anyway, not till my jaw stopped hurting.

DISCLAIMER (LAURA)

No Hodgson was harmed in the making of this book (neither punched nor slapped nor spoken to unkindly), though there were times I wanted to strangle him.

BERTIE AND JEEVES (BEN)

We got to talking about books again, and I gave her her first introduction to Wodehouse, *The Inimitable Jeeves*, which was the first one I had read. Subsequent inquiries revealed that she "hadn't gotten around to it, yet." Finally, one day she mentioned Bertie's purple socks and pink cummerbund, and Jeeves's disapproval, and I, knowing her penchant for letting cyberspace do her reading for her, suggested, "You could have got that much from the CliffsNotes." Then still later I grilled her, "How did Jeeves know that Harold the pageboy was such a fast runner?" She didn't get it exactly right, but close enough to convince me. Now if I can just get her to read *Brinkley Manor*, all will be right with the world.

COFFEE DATE (LAURA)

At the Casba Mediterranean Café, Ben opened a brown paper sack and set out two containers on the table: one piece of cherry cheesecake and a piece of apple pie. I didn't know whether he'd dumpster-dived these gifts or bought them with spare change, but either way it was a nice gesture. He wondered if the owner would mind if we ate the desserts since they weren't from the café, and I told him I would order a bowl of lentil soup. So far, the owner and his son had greeted us each week and I'd never felt any stink eye directed at our table by them or other diners. If anyone noticed the unwashed man wearing a dun-colored sweater cap and several layers of coats, they didn't let on. Ben had found a discarded stroller that he used for collecting cans, and this week we made a point of sitting next to the window so we could keep an eye on it. The week before, someone had made off with his bag of cans while we were inside.

Each week that passed brought winter closer, and our meetings took on a greater sense of urgency. Ben had been granted a much-coveted voucher to get into an apartment, but the addresses given to him by his caseworker all had waiting lists, some of them up to two years long. So the good news was that he had a waiver and the bad news was that he could still be camping for another year or more. His gear was pretty good, he assured me, and the tent in the southwest hills was warm enough at night.

He dialed an apartment near Laurelhurst Park and left a message on their voicemail.

"If you get any static from them," I said, "and you want me to call and have a conversation in a more dulcimer tone, just say the word."

"I think you mean dulcet, sweetheart," he said.

INVENTORY SPECIALIST (BEN)

Laura somehow found some space to store all the books in a building in the Pearl. Then she made me a job offer. Sort through the books and put them in some type of order. I was left in the basement, with just enough room to turn around (if I moved the books). There were a few half-filled shelves, arranged according to the way they came out of the boxes they'd arrived in.

I carved out some room on the back wall and tried to make some sense of it all. I was baffled, helpless. The questions frothed forth. Where shall I put them all? Do I go alphabetical by author or title? Don't we need more shelves? How in the world you supposed to do this? I settled on starting with two main halves. The good stuff, the car crashes and the explosions, on one side, Tolstoy and all them boring slobs on the other. I saw that if I beefed up the corners tight with books, I could transform the cardboard boxes into bookshelves. I stacked the boxes four across, then three, then two, and so on. I filtered out as many of the classics as I could uncover on the first pass and slowly assembled a pyramid library shelf, and then stepped back and admired my work. It didn't look half bad, and now there was a little room to move around in.

ECOTRUST (LAURA)

Our volunteer reference librarian, Beth, had a husband named Marc who worked at the Ecotrust building in the Pearl District. Thanks to him, sometime in late 2012 we wrangled some storage space there, downstairs in the basement. Suddenly I could move the tsunami of books from my basement at home. Now, when people reached out to us with offers to donate books, we had a place where we could meet them. In fact, the longer we stored books there and met folks for book handoffs, the more we felt a sense of belonging. The Pearl District had completed its metamorphosis from gritty industrial zone to leafy upscale neighborhood with boutique shopping and million-dollar lofts; we were essentially squatters among some of the city's wealthiest people. The librarian crew met weekly in the lobby at the tables next to the coffee cart, becoming a fixture at the place. It seemed that people assumed we worked somewhere in the building.

We were now an official 501(c)(3) with a fledgling board of directors. Establishing ourselves as a nonprofit meant that people could write off their donations to Street Books and that we would have an easier time applying for funding from foundations. Beyond that, I really didn't know what it meant.

CAMPSITE III (BEN)

I used a railroad spike to level the ground for my sleeping area. Maybe I should not have despoiled the landscape like that, but I jabbed the spike into the ground repeatedly to loosen it up, then moved the loose dirt to the low side. I would take a break from time to time, partly for the rest, and also to make room for the two robins that had their eyes on the worms I was digging up.

"No, no, you guys go ahead. Don't skimp on the worms for my benefit. You see, I am the kind of guy who has two or three worms and I'm done, so don't worry about me. Have all you want, take some with you."

It took me several sessions before I had it leveled out to my satisfaction, so the encounters with the robins went on for a few weeks. Then one day they had company. A couple of fledglings had come along. I don't know if the adults brought them over from the nest or what, but there they were. They could and did fly, but looked a bit clumsy doing so, and got around mostly by hopping. The robin family eventually moved on.

I wedged a shallow dish in a tree and put some hazelnuts in it, and soon had me a new pal. Birdbrain was a scrub jay that became a regular at the place, as long as I kept the nuts stocked. Mrs. Birdbrain would drop in as well. You could have stood them side by side and not been able to tell them apart, but it was easy to tell by the way they acted. Mrs. B.

would slip in carefully, look at me, then at the nuts, then back at me, then get a little closer, then check me again, then grab a nut and fly like hell out of there, usually colliding with a twig or two on the way out. All that for one hazelnut. Birdbrain was much bolder. He'd bop up to the dish and bolt about five or six nuts, then look at me like "Yeah, what of it?" then eat a few more and split.

Seems like in the city the only call you ever hear from a scrub jay is that aggressive screech they've got. Turns out they have a whole repertoire of songs. I never actually saw either of them singing, but I started to notice that I would hear it for a couple of minutes, and then Birdbrain would show up. Evidence but no proof, and I could not be certain that it was them until I looked it up at the library. I learned that there is a particular variety of jay that has an extended repertoire and is also an accomplished mimic. I felt vindicated.

The hazelnuts were cool for the scrub jays, but the sparrows had to settle for sunflower seeds and a mirror. I had a couple of makeup mirrors and I decided to put one in front of the seed dish to see how the birds handled it. It was like the slapstick comedies where the hero is in a difficult situation and everything he does to try and fix it only makes it worse. Only this was more fun to watch because it wasn't the movies, it was real. One bird would hop up to the mirror and peck at the other bird, then back off and wonder why it didn't leave. Tried it again and again, then got an idea. Hopped around behind the mirror to get that bird. Finding no bird, it hopped back to the seed dish. This bird would reenact that drama until I started to wonder if I wasn't just being cruel, since the bird had no chance of ever figuring it out. I finally decided that since the other bird wasn't harmed it didn't matter.

A deer and a fawn wandered in and out. Only once did a raccoon walk through. No squirrels at all. The moles had to have been there even if you never saw them. It was only the rats that came out. I kind of owe them something in a way because they did get me to thinking that I should take some responsibility for my actions. And since I was out there in a peaceful place with the time to reflect upon the vicissitudes of fortune, it finally dawned on me, in one of those rare moments of enlightenment, that it was probably mostly my own mistakes that had gotten me into this predicament. And only then was I able to realize that I had been slipping on the same banana peel ever since.

SHORTER DAYS (LAURA)

Ben turned us down a lot, even after we appointed him Inventory Specialist. We were still meeting for coffee once a week, but going downstairs to the book storage still seemed to be a little outside of what he was comfortable committing to. Finally he began to meet us at Ecotrust. He was thin and wan, and his raspy cough folded him in half when he laughed, but he moved around the space, pulling books from boxes and studying them, and every so often he put one on the shelf. He told me later that these work sessions were the highlights of his week, that he would soak up the humanizing conversation and then replay it later at his campsite. Sometimes he'd call me from his campsite with a joke to add or a follow-up story. It had been September when I reconnected with him. Still sunny and balmy some days. But as the leaves changed and the days grew darker, I knew that it was going to get harder for him to live outside. By winter I was very worried about him.

COLD (BEN)

It's not as unlivable as you might first think. But even in the dead of winter there were a couple times I cut my six-pack down to a four-pack and went to bed early because it was just too cold to sit outside my tent.

In *Heart of Darkness*, Joseph Conrad makes silence in the jungle its own character. Jack London does the same thing with the cold, like the ice in a beard. My first winter out in the cold, my friend Paul said, "You'll get used to it." I only half believed him at the time, but it turned out like he said. The cold comes on gradually and the body toughens up. Later, after I was back inside, I noticed it much more vividly. On the really nasty winter days, I would be downtown, bundled up as cozy as you please, but still feeling the bite of the cold and wind, wondering how I didn't hate it more when I lived outside in it. I remembered the Korean dude at the corner store who told me to have a cup of coffee on the house because it was cold outside. I suppose I should get over this kind of thing, but that sort of kindness still stops me in my tracks.

On one of our meetups at the coffee shop, Laura introduced me to Diana. We chatted for a bit and then I brought out the new limericks I had.

I went first:

To His Friend and Rival

Went over your book past few days
Really threw me into a malaise
Lost your book in the loo
Only thing I could do
To be rid of your shopworn cliches.

And then:

Order Form

So your inventory is deflicted
And some literature longs to be lifted
Call your old pal "the rooster"
Your number one booster
He's elusive, light-fingered, and gifted.

And then:

A Good Fit

The committee has come to its wits' end
In trying to find where he fits in
He's got really great looks
And writes pretty good books
Wha' we do with this guy Solzhenitsyn?

Diana must have decided that I was acceptable and Laura, bless her heart, handed me four dollars and said that I owed her four more limericks. Any excuse to help someone out.

It was so transparent that I had to laugh, but there's a lot you can do with four dollars, and I wasn't in any position to refuse. I got all four of them composed that same evening and voicemailed them over. You know, so that the four bucks would be legit.

FISH DINNER (LAURA)

The directions to the campsite were simple: Go to the Chart House restaurant in Southwest Portland. From the parking lot, head downhill past thirteen lamp posts, then take the trail to the right. Before long, I saw Ben waving at me from the edge of a clearing.

"Oh goody, you came," he said, and led me down the trail. The trees burned with autumn reds, rust, orange. The forest floor was golden with fallen leaves, and the air was crisp cold with filtered white sunshine. The campsite was hidden from view of the trail, and when I stepped into it, I saw it was swept clean with a little kitchen area and a dugout stove, plus a plastic basin and soap for washing dishes. There were knickknacks on a shelf, and two camp chairs set up on either side of a cooler doubling as a table.

Before I'd left home that morning, my husband Ben had caught me at the door.

"Hey," he said. "I know you trust this guy and everything, but do you mind turning on the Find My Friends app so I can see generally where you are today?"

"That's not a bad idea. Can you set it up?" I handed him the smartphone I'd recently inherited from him.

Now as I watched the other Ben stir up instant coffee and pour it into two chipped but clean mugs, my pocket buzzed with a text from Husband Ben that read "well, this is reassuring," along with a screenshot of a map showing that

I was located somewhere in the middle of the Willamette River.

"All good," I wrote back.

I had never gone to visit a Street Books patron before. Over the years I'd turned down a range of invitations. Everything from smoking weed at the waterfront to going upstairs to an apartment in the Park Blocks to view a guy's collection of books (at the time, I'd felt keenly that it was more than books he wanted to show me). But somehow, I knew without hesitation that I was safe with this Ben. He was rough around the edges, to be sure, but gentle at the same time. In that moment, I decided to call him Hodge, to keep the Bens sorted.

I watched him sprinkle creamer into our coffees. We clacked our mugs together and drank. After we finished, he gave me a tour of his campsite, pointing out a giant mushroom bigger than his outstretched hand, as well as the dedicated bird-feeding area, which included a frisbee to hold seed and a mirror for the birds to admire themselves while they ate.

For lunch he cooked pieces of white fish in a fry pan and garnished it with artichokes from a jar. He wouldn't let me help with the dishes.

PAYBACK (BEN)

Circadian rhythms. All animals have them, even plants do. From circa, meaning *about*, and dia, meaning *day*. About a day. And that's all it ever can be, is about a day, since the days themselves are constantly changing. Sleeping on the sidewalk in town, with all the noise and crowd and hassles making sleep difficult, you lose the feel of the rhythm. There's still a day and a night, but it seems like it's always a little off. Out at camp, after dark there's not a lot to do but call it a night. Quiet time all night, enjoying the sleep of the just, up and on the road well before sunrise. Even the roof dwellers don't get this much peace and quiet, but here I was getting a little slice of paradise. A little payback maybe for all that sidewalk shit.

LETTER

25 November 2013

Dear Honorable Judge:

My name is Laura Moulton. For the past three years, I have operated Street Books, a street library in Portland, serving people who live outside and lack the ID and proof of address required to check out books through Multnomah County's system.

In the summer of 2011, I had the opportunity to meet Ben Hodgson. He became a faithful patron, checking out books and returning them promptly, and spreading the word about Street Books to others. This summer I have been lucky to work with him again through the street library, lending him books and taking his recommendations for new titles.

Ben is knowledgeable and well-read and offers a lot to our project. We would like to offer him paid work in the coming year, and it is our hope that he will be allowed to resolve his outstanding warrant without doing any jail time. He has been approved for housing and is taking care of business.

Most sincerely,
Laura Moulton

BOARD (BEN)

Laura invited me to be on the board of Street Books and I asked how it was done. Did we all go to a graveyard at midnight on Halloween with a dead cat? And she said, "No cat ritual, we just say it's okay and then it is."

"Well good," I said. "Lucky for the cat, I guess."

WRITE THE MESSAGE (LAURA)

Pépe and I ran the shift at St. Francis on Tuesday. We set up across the street from a guy who was sorting through a giant pile of metal pieces. Each one crashed with a loud metallic sound when he'd drop it back onto the pile. A woman sat nearby, staring straight ahead through the din around her. Another woman walked around barefoot and covered in sores. I'd seen her before, but she had never stopped for a book and didn't respond when I spoke to her. The tents along 11th had been swept since our last shift. The residents were back, but with fewer belongings and now, no shelter.

A man in a black woolen peacoat stopped and took a careful look at each book. We talked about traveling. He told me he'd been in East Berlin shortly after the wall came down. One of his favorite books was *Down and Out in Paris and London*.

"In London, Orwell had people to fall back on, but in Paris it was real and kind of gritty," he said. "I prefer France."

We packed up the bike at the end of the shift and crisscrossed streets until we reached the Burnside Bridge. I pedaled slowly by a man I'd seen before. He was maybe in his thirties and dressed in layers of raggedy pants and several shirts and coats. He'd stopped me once earlier in the year to ask what date it was.

As I glided past him, I said hello.

"Excuse me," he said.

I stopped the bike. "Yeah?"

"Do you have a card?"

"Like, a Street Books card? We do." I hopped off the bike, opened the lid, and rooted around inside for minute. "Here it is."

"Thank you," he said. "Will you please write on it?"

I hesitated. "Write on it?" I searched my bag for a pen and then waited, poised above the card.

"Yes, please write the message 'pull up your pants, Takaharu.'"

I wrote what he asked and then handed him the card.

"Thank you," he said, then turned and shuffled away.

We crossed into Old Town and took a left on Second Avenue, leaving the rush of traffic behind us.

Pépe called to me over his shoulder. "What did he ask you?"

We rode along slowly and I told him. But as I described the exchange, I was thinking of something else entirely. I was thinking of how each of us has points of contact during our day, encounters with other humans that yield a kind of reliance on each other as a system of checks and balances. If people are alone, like Takaharu was, or at least appeared to be, it was possible that I was the sole point of contact for him that day. That week. That month? And so, his request for a reminder to pull up his pants? It was weird and unexpected, yes, but maybe it was also the message he most needed.

FAMILY TREE (BEN)

Another meeting at Ecotrust. Someone asked me if I had any kids, and I told them about Jennifer, who I had not seen in twenty-nine years or talked to for twelve. I didn't know if it was going to turn into a pity party. "Oh, you must miss her." "How sad." So I cut it short before it could start. "What I don't do," I said, "is worry about her. Whatever Jennifer is up to, she's doing something real good." And of course, I was right, as I so frequently am, but I did not know exactly how right I was and wouldn't find out for another two years. I did not know at that time that I had grandchildren. Imagine that, a grandfather for seven years and didn't know it.

WINTER (LAURA)

A skim of ice coated the car windows outside, and the water in the chicken coop and rabbit hutch had frozen overnight. In the early morning quiet, my kids still slept cozy in their beds. I thought of Hodge up in the hills and wondered whether his bedding and sleeping bag would be warm enough to get him through the winter. I knew he retired with a six-pack of Hamm's most nights and I worried he might freeze to death. He was so funny—the world needed his acerbic view.

I had written Hodge a letter for his visit to open court in Beaverton, where people went to turn themselves in for various outstanding warrants or fines. Hodge owed some money on a ticket for a DUI, something he wanted to make right. I asked the judge to allow Hodge to take care of things instead of serving the automatic thirty-day sentence that would result if he dropped out of sight and was eventually picked up again.

His day in court passed with no word from him. He didn't answer his phone when I called. Finally, I called Stephanie, his contact at the VA who had accompanied him. For confidentiality reasons, she couldn't tell me anything except that Hodge was okay. By the next evening, he'd phoned to say that the judge had given him a night in jail.

"But your letter helped," he said. "It didn't hurt."

LIFE SEEPED BACK IN (BEN)

Anyway, I outgrew it. Somehow life seeped back into me when I wasn't looking, and I was living outside and doing just fine. One night I was by the slab, where I never did sleep but there was usually a crowd there, and I had this sweater I thought someone might like to have. I was folding it up all ultra-neat-store-window style to make sure it would get noticed, when a guy came from all the way across the street and handed me three dollars and walked away. It was one of those little things that people do for no justifiable reason. Funny thing is, it was not the least bit humiliating. But it was humbling. There's a difference.

THREE

CREATURE COMFORTS (BEN)

It was such a rude shock getting exiled to the street. Not surprising, then, that moving back inside would also take some getting used to, and there are a few who mismanage the transition and end up back outside. Even more common are those whose new life of leisure allows them the time to drink themselves to death. Their only advantage: living out their last few years under a roof. Both my doctor and my case manager had seen it firsthand.

For me, the luxury had consequences, too. Like most do, I added a good fifteen pounds to my frame in about six weeks. I would sit around the apartment for a while, then start reading a book, then get drowsy and take another nap. My canning skills were still intact, so I could easily get beer money, but more often than not I'd be too lazy to even bother with it. Working once a week at the Street Books library also provided me with some funds.

One day there were three of us scheduled to meet but no one else was there when I arrived. After thirty minutes, I asked the coffee stand merchant if I might use her phone. She was kind enough to let me, but I got no answer. I gave it another fifteen minutes and then left, half suspecting that someone would get there soon after, which was precisely what happened.

The next Sunday was Easter, and I got a surprise visit from Laura and her daughter. They left me an Easter basket and I opened the egg to find some chocolate and thirty dollars that I had not earned shelving books but spent anyway.

Eventually I saw that without some cash in my pocket I was completely pinned down, so I made some arrangements and got a six-month assignment working with the groundskeeping crew at the national cemetery. My leg was still giving me trouble, and I was intensely unsure of myself and whether I could keep up and keep the job. Having been so isolated and out of circulation for so long didn't make it any easier, but I needn't have worried. There were a lot of veterans on the crew who were still feeling the aftershocks of their time overseas. That's part of what the program is for. They were very understanding and tolerant, but even so, there were a few that didn't last the six months. I managed to keep up a good enough pace, and more than just the money, it was, dare I say it, most therapeutic. Having a regular routine goes a long way towards bringing a sense of order to a life in disarray.

FIRST APARTMENT
BACK INSIDE (LAURA)

Hodge had an apartment now. Just saying it felt like magic: *Hodge's apartment.* No matter that it was slummy and a bit decrepit. Upper floor. Battered ten-speed on veranda.

He had decorated it with dumpster-dived items like taxidermied Armando and an ancient Spanish–English dictionary. There was a big, petrified wood wall hanging, a secondhand couch donated from the Home Forward program, and a clock with Roman numerals on the face—I couldn't remember if that was a dumpster score or a donation. The apartment was a one-bedroom and had a kind of splintery aesthetic. When Hodge gave me a tour, he pulled up a section of carpet to reveal a hole in the floor outside the bathroom. He'd gotten a mattress for the bedroom and stashed his gear in the closet. The stroller was there, the one he used to push around his big bags of cans and bottles.

After getting home the other day, he'd tossed his boots into the closet, and one had bumped a valve that caused water to leak onto the floor. It dripped for twelve hours without detection. Now, telling me about it, he shrugged. What could he do except tell the landlord and see what happened? While he seemed pretty unconcerned about the outcome, I was more attached than ever to keeping him indoors. It was February and Portland had seen both ice and snow in the past month.

CEMETERY (BEN)

On my very first or second day on the job, we were gathering in the vehicle area, sorting ourselves out, and I had one of my coughing fits, possibly smoking related, and one of the bosses looked at me and said, "Damn, dude, are you going to make it?" I shrugged it off with a weak smile and told him, "There's two schools of thought on that." He let it drop and we moved on.

Interesting job. Everybody knows about the flowers on the graves, but few ever think about what happens when they start to wilt. What happens is that eight or twelve of us went around and picked them up, once a week. Our first task of the day was to cover around one-fifth of the grounds every day, one section for each day of the week, excepting the one grave we left alone because the soldier's mom came out every day and took care of all that herself.

After two or three hours of that, and an hour or two of cruising around emptying all the trash cans, we finished out the day with a variety of jobs that came and went according to the season, and according to the day's workload. Weeding the flower beds was the most common side job. Not an everyday thing, but if the workload was light, any weed that had the audacity to come even a quarter inch out of the ground had to face the executioner.

It was on the weeding job that I started to notice Josh, this thirtyish-looking kid who never said anything, who wore a trench coat and a CamelBak, and looked for all the world exactly like a complete flipping fool. They had given him the nickname "Trench Coat." He was the sort of guy whose appointed destiny was to be a target of derision. We were on a weeding job when I first heard him speak. He was telling a story about William Shatner. How he had introduced a new line of lingerie, and that the business had failed. It turned out that there weren't many women interested in buying something called Shatner Panties. In that moment, I knew I had found a friend, derision be damned.

That weekend, Laura came by again, this time with her nine-year-old son along with her daughter. I got around to explaining my next million-dollar idea, which was a sundial with a digital readout. Laura gave no reaction, but the kid let out a snort at the absurdity of the notion.

"He got it!" I told her.

SEE WHAT HAPPENS (LAURA)

Owen wrote letters to televangelists, and over time lost his home and his wife. He wore tinfoil on his head to prevent access by the televangelists, who he was convinced had bugged his home. He talked about growing his own vegetables and the notion of being prisoners in our jobs. We don't get to be home with our spouses, he told me. Our only choice was to work all day to pay for the houses we were never in. And there were no good alternatives.

"Look at the homeless," he gestured around us. "So scraggly and dirty. Look at the choice that's offered you if you don't submit to a boss and work nine-to-five every day. See what happens when you don't kiss up to the Roman Empire?!"

CEMETERY II _(BEN)

The previous record was 1877. Before long, I saw the new record, born 1874. Served in the Spanish-American War. The markers said what war if the guy was in one. I'd seen maybe three or four Spanish-American War markers, nothing earlier. Very few WWI, but WWII, the Korean War, and Vietnam were not uncommon at all. Lt. Col. Robert I. Hodgson is one such.

The newer ones, as you might imagine, had the most flowers to clear off. Somebody had to pick them up, and they set it up so they got picked up the day that section got mowed, so that the lawnmower drivers didn't have to stop and do it. That's when we had the time to look at the markers. Tan Quoc Ngo, obviously a Vietnamese dude, killed in Afghanistan at the age of twenty. And why on earth a Vietnamese guy wanted to go fight for the United States, well, the "melting pot," I guess. He was as American as anyone else.

Josh was into checking for odd names. You know, Willie Maykit, Betty Wont, stuff like that. I saw Woodrow Wilson over in section V. Born 1917, and since their family name was already Wilson, they musta figured, why not Woodrow? I found an odd name for Josh to check out in section II. A name odd as odd can possibly get. Odd. A name cannot get any more odd than Odd, unless it's Odd Roar. Odd Roar Enestreeth. What were mommy and daddy thinking? It reminded me of Bunny Cottonwood and Stormy Knight from when my family lived in Beatty, Nevada.

We did section V on Tuesdays. Our old family friend Frankie was there. I'd been stopping by to say hi the last few weeks. They just put "Francis A. Campbell" on the marker. Francis Arthur Patrick Campbell would have fit on the stone, but I guess the stonemason decided that would be a bit excessive.

Want to make it weird and spooky? Only by looking at the stone did it occur to me that the day Frankie died was on my daughter Jennifer's sixteenth birthday. My sister Bonnie was killed when she was sixteen. When I stood at the grave, I still did not know that I was a granddaddy. Jennifer's firstborn, name of Franky, was seven. Tallulah Isabel was five. Growing up too fast with many milestones ahead of them. Me, standing here, with gravestones ahead of me.

REMISSION (LAURA)

Outside of St. Francis, a tiny, wizened woman stepped toward me for a hug and then did a double take.

"Hey, you're not Diana!" she said.

"I'm Laura. I'm subbing for Diana this week."

"I'm Constance." She shook my hand with both of hers. "When you see Diana, tell her I'm in remission."

It wasn't the first time I'd been mistaken for Diana, but I didn't mind. She was an empathetic listener who remembered everyone's story. "I'll do that," I said.

Just then, a man ran whooping and hollering across the grass. "The puppies are coming!" he yelled.

"I gotta go," Constance said. "I'm the vet for the animals around here."

My student, Spencer, was there observing the shift that day. He was also helping me organize and display books on the bike. I knew a couple things about him: He'd grown up Mormon like I had, and the year before, his husband had undergone brain surgery. Spencer was also a very fine writer. When Constance dashed off to go assist with the puppies, she'd grabbed him by the arm and taken him along.

The whole thing blew his mind. Later that week in class, he confessed that he felt like a terrible person to admit this, but the experience had been a visceral punch in the face. He said that the people at the van had welcomed him heartily and pushed him closer to look inside, where tiny puppies were squirming along their mother's side. The van interior with its heaps of clothing and smell of bodies had left Spencer woozy. He told the class he'd gone home and taken two showers.

"I know I'm fastidious," he said, "but it was just very far outside my comfort zone."

I told the class that I had no agenda when it came to them visiting the library shifts. They didn't have to share my opinions about the people who lived outside and visited the library each week. The important part was their willingness to leave their comfort zones, and see the ways people were human, no matter their circumstances. Maybe these encounters could shift our thinking on subjects we thought we knew the answers to.

While Constance and Spencer were away at the van, I stood at the book bike and watched another scene unfolding at the curb. An ambulance had arrived with no siren, though the light on its roof was spinning. A man with long white hair and a beard was helped onto a stretcher, then loaded into the back.

A patron looking through our selection turned and waved as the man disappeared into the ambulance.

"We're with you, Bill," he called.

DIFFERENT WORLDS (BEN)

If you try to bring the street with you into your brand-new apartment it's just not going to work. It's two different worlds, and ne'er the twain shall meet. My neighbor Kim told me about someone who made it off the street but not quite. She said this woman was throwing a big party at her place, and she had had about enough, or maybe a little too much. She needed to get to bed, but with the party going on she couldn't find a place to do it. She went out to her car and crashed in the back seat. When she woke up, she was in the lot at a tow yard. She hadn't gotten the correct parking sticker for that apartment, and the tow company had carte blanche to patrol the parking lots of all the apartments in that end of town. Pretty funny, isn't it? No, it is not. The funny part is that this was the second time this had happened to her.

CROSSING PATHS (LAURA)

At the corner of Fourth and Burnside, I set the brake on the bike and pulled out the drawer to display the books for the R2D2 shift. As I stepped back to inspect my work, I nearly bumped into a man passing by, and missed what he'd just said.

"Sorry, what was that?" I asked.

As soon as I turned to look into his eyes, I realized that he had been blazing his own path and having his own conversation, which I had unfortunately stepped into. This had nothing to do with me.

"Fuck. You. Bitch," he said, and the last word sounded like he'd torn it in half on its way to me. He kept walking in the same jagged direction and didn't look back.

My heart skipped. It took my breath a little, leaving me shaken for the rest of the afternoon. This kind of encounter was rare at the library. I trusted it would never become routine.

REPERTOIRE (BEN)

Sometimes after board meetings, Laura would drive me to a bus stop that was close to her house, and we'd get to talking.

"I saw some guy hustling out of the Safeway with a six-pack, trying to get away on a pogo stick."

"Wow, that's weird."

"Really weird."

"How far did he get?"

"I don't know. I was on the bus and only saw it for a few seconds. Then the store manager came out and started chasing him on a pogo stick."

"Hey, wait a minute. Isn't today the first of April?"

"Huh? No, it's March 32nd."

NOTE TO SELF II (LAURA)

We had a Street Books board meeting and Hodge came and it seemed like he might have had alcohol on his breath. I wasn't sure. But I really hope he's okay—he's had a sudden turnabout of fortune, in some ways, meeting up to do book sorting with us, then going to visit the filmmakers, Anne Rosellini and Debra Granik, a couple days ago. They were looking at making a film about Peter Rock's fictionalized account of the father-daughter duo discovered living up in Portland's Forest Park. I introduced them to Hodge, and they asked him many questions over several hours at Floyd's Old Town Coffee Shop. He was a bit subdued, shy with them. Definitely more deferential than I'd seen him in a while. Still wearing his horn-rimmed glasses with the tape around the middle. Apparently not because there is something broken about the glasses, but because he likes the aesthetic.

He'd written a list of names that went from the top to the bottom of a sheet of paper. "Behind each one of these is a story," he said.

NOT A LIMERICK (BEN)

It is partially analogous to your old hypothalamus
A failure to blossom in the corpus callosum
When all your endorphins have gone to the orphanage
And your whole limbic system is crimping your vision
You've arrived at the junction of thought and dysfunction

Or maybe you're just tired.

BLINDERS (LAURA)

Suddenly I realized that I'd been like a decorated little horse, clip-clopping on parade with those black blinders on, the ones designed to keep me from getting spooked and bolting into the crowd. The blinders were the narrative I'd built around Hodge that was pure redemption story—yes, there was bound to be darkness there, but in the end he had saved himself, was funny and wry and self-deprecating and fond of us, devoted to Street Books. Never missed a meeting, always showed up early. Whatever had dogged him in his past was bound to be neatly resolved—just a court fee to pay off, or a family relationship to repair. But up till now, I hadn't seen the grubby dark it could be.

I went to his house for a writing session, and the room was a wall of cigarette smoke, butts and ash in a little pile on a table, him pacing and rambling. He was worried about his brother, Mike, who had been in the hospital and was quite sick.

He handed me his notebook. "Good thing I skipped Humanities class last night, because get a load of this writing I managed to produce."

I bent over the page and read short bursts of vitriol, veering toward paranoia. None of what I read sounded like him. This was not the Hodge I knew. He was so off that I suddenly felt like I didn't know what he might do next. I gathered my things and got out of there.

I didn't know much about mental illness. By then I had served many people over the years who were clearly ill, but they either pulled it together enough to check out a book, or hollered or frothed or limped past, deep in discussion with a shadow nobody else could see. I hadn't been up close like this before, where I saw the illness taking someone I knew away from me. He was reduced to pacing and smoking furiously and tossing the cigarette when it was halfway done. (That's how I knew he was really sick, when he wasted a perfectly good cigarette.)

He was shaky when he met Diana and me for coffee the following week, apologetic and anxious. Jittery hands, smoked a lot out at the curb.

I wondered how often I'd seen symptoms of his illness without recognizing them, or given him a pass because by then he'd become beloved. My definition of what was strange, or what was considered "crazy" had been blown wide open after Street Books. I dunno. Hodge said, "Laura, you are a lighthouse because you save people, and you're a unicorn too."

LIMERICK (BEN)

Gonna get me an apartment in town
Be responsible, not just a clown
Be a force in society
Even practice sobriety
Naw, screw that, I'll just see you around.

MR. HODGE'S
NEIGHBORHOOD (LAURA)

I was thinking about how Hodge has helped so many people since he transitioned back into housing, into his apartment. Like the kid, Isaiah, who showed up after being run over by a cement truck, and slept for fourteen hours on the couch, took a shower, felt human again. Sometime after he'd left, Hodge realized Isaiah had come back while he was away, reaching through the back door to unlock it, and helped himself to Hodge's loaf of bread and peanut butter. Hodge was nonplussed, but I was a bit inflamed on his behalf. It's not like he's rich in groceries himself.

But then there was the repeat offender, Tom, sort of a foul fellow who kept coming back. Hodge would always let him in to sleep off a drunk or take a shower. Finally he stopped answering the door. Then there was the manic stage where he was hosting the couple who'd lost their RV (and all worldly possessions) when it had been towed, and Hodge suggested that maybe Street Books could buy the RV and get it out of hock, and I said we weren't really entitled to use the funds that way. The couple lived in Hodge's back bedroom with their dog and became somewhat terrible houseguests over time, until he must have encouraged them to move on, but not before I grew anxious that he would jeopardize his own shelter in the service of someone else.

Today, it's Hodge and me going to compete for a grant from the Awesome Foundation, a philanthropic group that gives out $1,000 grants with no strings attached. I hope they'll fund us. So funny, the distance we've traveled together. He's one of my best friends and he's also crazy.

SPOKESMODEL (BEN)

Laura and I had gotten there early, so we had time for a brief strategy session. I'd be the game-show lady, à la Carol Merrill or Vanna White, and as Laura gave the presentation, I was to run my fingers invitingly down the spine of the book, making it look all kinds of sexy. I knew, of course, that it was degrading and exploitative, but since it was for a good cause, I didn't mind. And then I reasoned that if the sex object thing worked out for me, maybe I could quit my job at the cemetery. It went well. We were the fifth of five pitches, and I don't know if anyone else noticed, but we ran a little over the three-minute limit and they didn't cut us off, so I guess going last did give us at least some edge. It certainly wasn't my being there that tipped the balance our way, but I enjoyed my contribution all the same.

GENTRIFIED (LAURA)

That spring, a new block of food carts opened up on the corner near Hodge's apartment. Sure enough, by July there was a notice on his door.

LOOKING FOR A NEW PLACE (BEN)

When the food carts went up at SE 72nd and Foster, I knew I would have to move sooner or later. The mayor had declared a housing emergency and was requiring landlords to give a sixty-day notice instead of the usual thirty-day notice. The landlords were clever and gave the notice thirty days sooner than they would have otherwise, and so it amounted to very much the same thing.

My caseworker Jarvis was impressed that I had called it before it happened. I'm not at all sure that I could have found another place without his magic. We drove around looking for likely apartments, and after a few days came to this one spot. It took some looking to find the office, and even the mighty Jarvis was pleased when he figured out who he was talking to. "You're Cathy?" He knows a lot of apartment managers, but never having placed anyone in this complex, had only heard the name. Most apartment managers get so many calls every day asking about vacancies that they don't bother with a waiting list. He gave Cathy his card and said, "Maybe we can think of this as your first phone call of the day for about thirty days?"

NEW APARTMENT (LAURA)

Hodge waited until we were sitting down for a coffee at Ecotrust to tell me that he had a new apartment to move into. This one was in North Portland. It would be close to Diana and her family, which was a win.

"That's such good news," I said. "If everything is settled then, maybe it's time we wrote some grants and did some projects. Any ideas? Schemes?"

"Some kind of event?" he said. "How about we write a grant for a Homeless Olympics and we run it along the waterfront?"

"A Homeless Olympics?"

"Yeah, like with different events: a shopping cart race, the backpack grab. Maybe a citywide panhandling competition?"

"I was thinking something more like you write your stories down and we capture them in a book."

Hodge was so funny and smart. His jokes were often noxious, but by now I felt the larger message of his goodness needed to be in the world, so that his brilliance was recognized instead of his time spent as a "homeless puke," as he liked to put it. We'd recently published essays in *Street Roots*, printed on opposing pages, as though in dialogue. Mine was called "What I learned from Ben" and his title was a nod to the Orwell that he'd borrowed from me back at the end of the first season.

"What if we take turns writing our story? You, then me," I said. "We can alternate points of view and try to tell how it happened from the very beginning."

Hodge shrugged. "We could also do that."

TEXT EXCHANGE

B: Maybe I just had a great idea for a story. Have often wondered where the books end up once they go out. Well, in this story, five books end up in an encampment. And they get to swapping stories about their misadventures amongst the houseless. Maybe have the titles reflect the tales, like maybe Denisovich had a tougher time of it, or the western talks real tough. They may have changed owners two or four times, so any imbroglio you can cook up would fit. Whatcha think??

L: YES! Please write a draft of that tonight and show me tomorrow.

B: Don't let's rush things. Anyway, *you* s'posed to write it.

EMAIL TO HODGE

I've been thinking about how to write a Street Books book, what to include, how to describe the experience without feeling like I'm appropriating others' stories. (This is something that has shut me down a few times, the fear of appropriation.)

One idea would be that you and I can write something together and lean on the street library as the framework. As in, we can both talk about crossing paths, and then talk about what happened in between seeing each other again. Then get at everything that has happened since. Are you in?

EMAIL TO LAURA

Have your people call my people; we'll do lunch. Love your hair, baby, don't change a thing.

NOTE TO SELF III (LAURA)

Hodge and I are working on the Street Books book. We'll do a reading from it in October, and then we'll figure out what to do with it. We're still filling in the blanks. I bought him a little green cactus with a red top on it, like a crown. Told him its name was Travis. He is funny and odd and wonderful, as always. Diana and I compare notes on whether he's edging toward a manic energy (this could be the season, if we're going in cycles), but for now I think he's holding steady. Still drinking beers at night instead of medicating with prescription drugs. Can still be relied on to produce bad puns and jokes.

He's into his new apartment, which is good, but yesterday when we arrived for a visit, he sang "All Around the Mulberry Bush" and skipped in place when he opened the door, and my heart sank. He has all the symptoms on the website I looked at yesterday:

- Sleeping less
- Elevated mood
- Restlessness
- Speaking rapidly
- Increase in activity level
- Irritability or aggression

LETTER FROM NATALIE

Laura,

My name is Natalie. I am the niece of Ben Hodgson. I wanted to thank you for your beautifully written article on my uncle. It is nice to know that during the years he was on the street and disconnected from his family he had kind people like you who looked beyond his living situation and got to know him as the smart, witty person we know.

During the last four years there were times when we didn't really know if he was dead or alive. When I would find myself in Portland I would always wonder if I would run into him near the Mission on Burnside. It always hurt me to know the stigma that is attached to people who live on the streets. That people would look at someone who is probably better read than themselves and write them off as simply a loser.

Thank you for challenging people to look beyond their first impressions.

I know you are probably an extremely busy person. I thought it wouldn't hurt to ask if you'd ever be available to speak to a high school class. I'm teaching Health at a local high school in Vancouver, Washington. We are starting to transition into a unit on stress and then mental illnesses. I thought it would be interesting for someone like you to discuss what you have learned about people living on the streets. I know most people who are homeless are battling mental illness, like my uncle. I think lessons like this would really help the students understand that most people don't choose that life; more is going on within themselves that they are battling.

Thanks again,
Natalie

WRITING A BOOK (BEN)

My first section is called "Équipage Pathétique," which is the right euphemism for depression. And various references to a lack of joie de vivre.

An absence of, a shortage. How the high point of my "seeing the beauty in all things" was noticing how that square of cracked sidewalk looked like the state of Idaho. Several times a day for a lot of days. In other words, make it funny to ameliorate the pathetic.

COMPOSITION

B: Hey, you cut out the bit on the first page about the mole climbing out of the pile of garbage.

L: I left one mole reference but cut out the second because it's repetitive.

B: Yeah, but the repetition is intentional, see? It's *intentionally* bad writing. That's the funny part.

L: But how are our readers supposed to know you were writing badly on purpose? We'd have to create a footnote or insert a whole conversation about it for them to know.

NEW SHOES (LAURA)

Hodge turned sixty-two. We went to the Hollywood Fred Meyer and bought him a new pair of shoes. They were hip, kind of like a generic version of Vans. Outside the store, he leaned against a garbage can for balance and stepped out of the old sneakers he'd worn for three and a half years while living on the streets.

He laced up the new ones and took a few steps in each direction, admiring them. The old shoes looked forlorn on the sidewalk where he'd left them. They had holes and the sole on one of them had come loose so that it flopped when he walked. He picked the shoes up and pushed them into a garbage can.

He was settled in his new place now and called me some evenings after I was already asleep, leaving voicemails full of oddball, funny stuff. One night he told me that he'd met a man at the Mission, a person so funny, so charming that he threatened to unseat me as Best Friend. But Hodge said not to worry.

"Second place is not so bad."

He told the man all about Street Books and offered him a place to crash if he needed it. The guy took him up on his offer and lay down in the bedroom. Hodge apparently just kept right on talking to him (the mania makes for a lot of monologues, it turns out) because eventually he heard the guy say, "Leave me alone, I'm in pain."

The next day, Hodge left me another voicemail, letting me know that the guy was still asleep, more than fourteen hours later.

He was almost reverential when he told the story. "Imagine how tired this guy must have been."

AUTOBIOGRAPHY (BEN)

By the time I was eighteen, I had lived at twenty different addresses in four states. Not a military family, but a ramblin' scramblin' one. Not dirt poor, but mostly broke as a joke. I guess you could say I was born to ramble but kept coming up a little short on the bus fare.

Having nothing else to compare it to, I obviously didn't know the difference. One thing that does start to happen is you begin to detect a pattern in the cast of characters in whatever spot you find yourself. Vonnegut claims that you never leave high school. Twenty years later in the office, and there they all are, the clique of cool kids, the jocks, the dorks, the brains, the dopers, the bully, even the cheerleaders.

As the youngest in a large family, the first object lesson in life was to learn the fine art of staying out of the way. It became so ingrained in me that it is my habit to this day. And being out of my depth on the conversational plane, I didn't speak ten words together to anyone before I was eight. I didn't say much after that, either.

It was around ninth or tenth grade that I first hit my mainline with my favorite drug, which was watching all the comedians on the TV variety shows, from Steve Allen to Richard Pryor. My brother and I would stay up to watch Johnny Carson's monologue and then go to bed, unless there was another comic coming on later. If I have ever gotten anything right it was by happenstance, because the only thing I ever wanted to be was funny, and I think I came close.

RAIN (LAURA)

The world came down in sheets of rain and the Pearl District filled up, flooding cars and basements. We got word from Ecotrust that everyone was checking the downstairs locker spaces for water, so I donned rain boots and made my way to the Pearl. Hodge met me, and then Diana came, and we discovered that the water had risen to the edge of some boxes of books. Two boxes were slightly damp, but no books were damaged.

Hodge was soaked, wearing his extra-thick, black horn-rims (the ones with the tiger-print tape wrapped around the middle). The glasses made his eyes look especially big. He was wearing a hat with a pilot-ear-flap thing going on. He carried a wet, brown paper bag with newspapers inside, plus a gift for Sylvie: a still life painting of flowers and a drawing of a cyclops.

He was out of money (having been giving it away) and out of most food, near as I could tell. For a week he'd been hosting a man named Gary.

I gave him twenty dollars because he was out of ciga-rettes and that was really killing him. I said it was from me, personally, and not Street Books—I told him our nonprofit couldn't bankroll his cig habit.

SHOULD I TELL IT (BEN)

I rode the bus to Marylhurst for one of Laura's night class-es, and I read from my *Street Roots* article, then answered questions. One of her students wanted to know if Laura ever encountered someone who made her uneasy, especially since she was hanging a shingle out in the midst of the disen-franchised, drawing attention to herself. And compare and contrast that to me, and whoever made me uneasy. It was the kids giving the teacher an essay question.

I asked Laura if she remembered the mythology girl, and should I tell it. Yes and yes she said. So I told them. There was a young lady, obviously very happy, who waltzed and pirouetted around the library premises and asked about a mythology book. We may or may not have been uneasy, in the same way that she may or may not have had more than just blood in her bloodstream. I looked for a mythology title or related subject, and, finding neither, quickly sug-gested she might prefer something else. She looked at us with her larger eye and said, "Do you know what was left in Pandora's box after all the troubles of the world flew out?" I didn't know, and I looked at Laura and she didn't know. "It was hope," she said. "Hope and hope alone. All by itself." And she waltzed off, leaving us with nothing.

SUCCESS STORY (LAURA)

My notion of a success story, and my understanding of what constitutes a happy ending has changed over time. Take for example this girl named Roxie. One morning, I checked out a new book to her and we had a great conversation. Later that afternoon, when I packed up the bike library to move on, I saw her sitting against a wall, unable to hold up her head. And seeing that, I'd felt a little crushed, but why? Did I think the paperback I'd loaned her would solve all her problems? After so many years, I'd learned to accept that these things could coexist alongside one another. That is, a girl could check out a novel in the morning from a street library and be in a heroin nod by lunchtime. It didn't mean our conversation hadn't counted. Maybe the success part of the story came when she'd spotted me from a distance that morning and come running across the square to return the book she'd borrowed last week.

VONNEGUT (BEN)

It was about halfway through the season and I was looking over the selections. I picked up a copy of *Bluebeard* and studied the back cover. "Do you read much Vonnegut?" Laura wanted to know. I dropped the book and said, "Right now I just vanna get out of here." And she slapped me.

GAINFUL EMPLOYMENT (LAURA)

Like I said, no Hodge was harmed in the making of this book. If it was occasionally hard to predict what version of Hodge might show up, we knew for certain that he always arrived when he said he would, usually early. When it came time to draw up the schedule for the summer season, it made sense to assign Hodge the Old Town Chinatown beat. He knew the territory better than any of us and now he'd return to his old haunts with books to lend.

UNLIKELY CHECKOUTS (BEN)

In the fifth year of Street Books, I started showing up at the shifts as a second pair of hands and mostly because it was my best chance to see my friends. I think that was the last year of the solo shifts, once we all saw how much easier it was with a sidekick. I would find either Diana or Laura at R2D2, or the Worker Center, or St. Francis. One day, I brought *Nineteenth Century Russia* with me, knowing that it would be a tough sell, which it was. After a few more visits, it was Diana who finally checked it out.

I tried to bring something for every taste. I knew that Peter Lovesey's *Wobble to Death* had only the tiniest market niche out there. It was a murder mystery that took place at a wobbling event. The sport of wobbling, an indoor track-walking marathon where the last walker standing takes all. Turn of the century England. The first checkout was easy; I forced it on someone. Took it back the next time I saw them, and later that same day came across a guy who was a huge fan of the BBC and wanted to read the thing. You just never know.

I kind of made it my shtick or whatever to try and promote the hard-to-place books. Cherie Calbom's *Juicing for Life*, for example, while a fascinating book in its own way, is a real tough sell to people who do not have a juicer. But someone did eventually check it out. *The Arms of Krupp* by William Manchester also has a limited appeal, but as I was pitching it to the guy on my left, the guy on my right said, "Hey, let me see that." Turned out he knew a lot about the Krupps and their centuries-old armament business.

The John Dewey book, on the other hand, was always going to be a struggle. *The Child and the Curriculum*, as you can see, is targeting a very exclusive readership. "One of our more overlooked thinkers," is how I began my pitch. And we did check it out, but it doesn't count. It was a couple, and he wanted to leave, but she wanted him to get a book, so he asked if we had any nonfiction and I said, well there's this, and without even looking at it, he took it. No count. He even returned it later, but I don't think he read it. I know I wouldn't have.

And the self-help books. I read a few of them in my day. I suppose I got a couple of fresh ideas from them. I suppose the ones they got now do about the same thing, if you find the right one, which we did. It was by Francesco Marciuliano, called *You Need More Sleep: Advice from Cats*. A picture of a cat on the cover, looking pleased.

OBSERVATION (LAURA)

One thing I began to think about with every library shift I operated was that people generally take great pains not to draw attention to themselves. Seems like most everybody prefers not to have the world looking at them. So much so that by the time a person arrives at the idea of holding a cardboard sign, you can guess that something major has broken. And by the time they have decided to linger at the MAX train station, or at Skidmore Fountain, or in a park, screwing up their courage and asking people for change, expecting to be refused, anticipating perhaps even some abuse, they have let go of the impulse to pretend that things are fine, when they are definitely not fine.

STREET LIBRARIAN (BEN)

Rachel and I were teamed up for a season, and we had to make it up as we went along, deciding where to set up. We figured we'd give Elephant Park a try. We set the bike up next to the elephant and waited. And waited. There were people out there, in pockets of threes and fours, on benches, on the turf, but no takers. We needed to circulate and drum up some business. And I noticed I was nervous and apprehensive about doing it, which was strange, because I had lived out here, so why should I be nervous? But I was. So it was with some trepidation that I put a couple of books in each hand as a prop, and made the rounds. "We got a book bike over there, you want to see?" And it got a little bit of a response, so we stuck with the spot for the rest of the season.

SELF-CARE (LAURA)

Hodge told me he'd commenced an exercise regimen, jogging loops around the field at Ockley Green Middle School, slowing to a walk only when he couldn't breathe anymore.

I tried my best to picture him working out. "You got running shoes?"

He shrugged. "I've got my boots. And I run in them. So yeah, more like running boots."

He also filled a prescription from his doctor for Wellbutrin, which was supposed to help him stop smoking. It wouldn't give him the will to stop so much as it would cause him to lose the taste for cigarettes altogether. There were side effects to watch out for, so he asked me to keep an eye on him, in case I noticed him doing anything untoward, or unusual.

"That's a tall order, Hodge," I told him. "Trying to identify something odd about your behavior."

He looked at me over his glasses. "You know what I mean."

To stand next to Hodge when he coughed or laughed was to listen to an involuntary excavation, the scraping of shovels, the shifting of something deeply internal. Once, when I saw a young street librarian lighting up, I said, "If you ever want to kick that habit, stand next to Hodge when he laughs." She grimaced. *I know.*

At home, I searched online for possible side effects of Wellbutrin, and found that when combined with alcohol, the drug can cause hallucinations, delusions, paranoia, mood changes, depression, suicidal thoughts, anxiety, and panic attacks. It occurred to me that I'd known Hodge to experience some of those things on his own. And there was this: For all the time I'd known him, Hodge had adhered closely to beer-thirty, which meant that each evening, he'd be washing down the Wellbutrin with a six-pack of Hamm's.

"I'll watch you," I told him.

SHAKESPEARE (BEN)

The first shift I did by myself I set up at Red Doors, where the early birds start showing up an hour or more before they open, and the line runs up Burnside from Sixth to Broadway and around the corner.

I didn't even get set up before a couple of people started looking through the shelf. It was a fairly busy ninety minutes, and then a guy came by asking if I had any Shakespeare. I was sure I recognized him as the same guy who had asked us twice before for Shakespeare, at different locations. Limited shelf space or no, the third time you have to say, "No, we don't have any . . . don't believe I ever heard of that fella," was one time too many. The prospect of disappointing him yet again bothered me. So, desperate times called for desperate measures.

I had a set of the *Great Books of the Western World* that'd been largely unread for quite some time, and I got both Shakespeare volumes and brought them with me to St. Francis the next Thursday. I went inside and looked around and spotted him. He had a bunch of notebooks open, with his writings in them. I said, "Are you the guy that was asking about Shakespeare?" Yes, he was. "Okay, here's two volumes. The complete works. Now you wanna stop making us look bad for a while?" Talked to him for a bit. He referred to Shakespeare as "the best junk you can get."

ODES OF MARCH (LAURA)

I challenged the street librarians to participate in the Odes of March, which meant we would be writing an ode each day for the first fifteen days of the month and sending them to each other via email. I composed an ode to the rain, an ode to the giant maple outside my window, and an ode to Black Black the chicken, buried in the yard. She'd lived to the age of thirteen, which the kids were convinced was a world record. I only made it to day six of the ode writing, but it turned out everyone else had abandoned it already. Odes were hard. They required one to praise and celebrate and glorify a thing, to enter into a kind of rapture. This kind of sentiment, it turned out, is not very sustainable.

On day three, Hodge sent a limerick instead:

> You are two steps ahead down ode road
> And I fear I have shirked off the load
> ·I am steeped in such sorrow
> But I'll write one tomorrow
> And that is the ode that is owed.

I met his limerick, and raised him one:

> Regarding your moods, I'll be wary
> With smoking cessation, don't tarry
> We like you a bunch
> We'll take you to lunch
> Provided you're not too contrary.

When I read it to him over the phone, he laughed. Then he coughed. Then he laughed some more.

THE PITCH (BEN)

I made it back to Red Doors the next Monday, but there was a closed sign on the window, so I decided to scout out new locations. As I was rolling down Third, I heard someone call out, "Street Books, I want a book." So I backed up and opened the lid. I had known all along that the knitting and crocheting book was gonna be a tough sell, but I thought I'd give it a try with the folks who'd stopped me. So I picked it up and started in with, "This could just be your lucky day, we have right here . . . in one book . . . most of what you need to know about knitting and crocheting." I swear, it's the truth. The guy said, "Hey, my girlfriend is all into knitting and crocheting, let me get that one." The other guy got a Louis L'Amour, and the third person of the group, Beatrice, got something for herself. I remember rolling by that same block later, and I don't know where they got brooms, but I saw two different people sweeping up all around their tent.

I tried the waterfront and the South Park Blocks, but mostly it was too early and deserted. I got over to Blanchet House at about eleven fifteen and set up by the front door so everybody knew I was there. Then, as soon as they opened the door at eleven thirty, I hustled back around to the exit door, where there was a small but steady stream trickling by. Now, this wasn't like Red Doors, where you had a captive audience. Lunch was over and everybody could just leave, so I went into carnival barker and all-around pitchman mode,

"Hey, step right up and get the story. We got short stories, long stories, true stories, love stories, war stories, and morning glories. We put it in words, in sentences, paragraphs, and entire chapters. And because it's such a nice day, we're gonna throw in the punctuation marks, for nothin'."

GOOD FORTUNE (LAURA)

Hodge and I ate pot stickers and green beans at the Golden Horse, his favorite Chinese place in Old Town. We broke open our fortune cookies and pulled the papers out.

"Okay," I said. "Whatever these say will be advice for us about our book."

"You're not one of those I Ching throwers, are you?" he said.

I confessed that once upon a time back in the day, when my Ben and I had been trying to decide a next step in life, we'd thrown his mom's I Ching and consulted her book to find our future.

IT FURTHERS ONE TO CROSS THE GREAT WATERS, it had read. And so we'd followed the advice and moved to Taiwan together.

"That's a big leap to take because of a couple of coins," Hodge said.

My fortune read: TRUST YOUR HUNCHES. THEY'RE USUAL-LY BASED ON FACTS FILED AWAY JUST BELOW THE CONSCIOUS LEVEL.

Hodge's: ONE'S MIND, ONCE STRETCHED BY A NEW IDEA, NEVER REGAINS ITS ORIGINAL DIMENSIONS.

KEEPING THE PEACE (BEN)

Diana was set up at St. Francis one day when a debate broke out. As it escalated toward the physical, she decided that discretion might be the key to staying in one piece and started putting the books away. Then one guy held up a restraining hand and said, "Could you hold on a minute, please? I didn't get my book yet." He hurled a final insult at his interlocutor and brought his better self over and started looking through the shelf.

Most people on the street don't even bother looking up when the arguments flare, and it's the exception if it ever goes any further. To them, it's only slightly more rough-and-tumble than the average schoolyard. There was a guy that had really bad taste in clothes, to the point where he didn't have any, and even with that outrage, no one did anything to him. Someone did walk his pack over to the river and toss it in, but that's not violence, just damage.

And the older guy on the bike with the good music must have been at least partly right if he was willing to stand alone across from a crowd of five. The crowd couldn't hardly gang up on an old guy, so the young girl walked over and knifed a hole in his tire. Damage, not violence; the man was never touched.

One night, back when I still lived outside, I was ready to get some sleep when some drunk started getting aggressive with anyone within earshot. I was defenseless and don't even know if I would have had the sense to run if he had come any closer. Someone else asked for quiet and that was all the drunk needed to shift it into high gear, but then someone else quickly added, "Hey dude, you're messing with the wrong homeboy," and that was all it took. The drunk backed right down and left. Simple when you know how.

BATTERY (LAURA)

Hodge and I met at the Killingsworth Library and he told me a story about Tom, the guy who comes and crashes with him sometimes. Hodge knew him from back when he was also sleeping outside—I think they had met at a shelter or the Mission or something. Over the winter, when Hodge had been in high mania, he'd been extra generous, and invited people home to stay with him. Tom had been one of his guests. And apparently he'd slept for three days straight when he first arrived. Anyway, once Hodge came down a bit, settled, and was steadier, he noticed that every time Tom came through to crash at his place they'd get really plastered and Hodge would lose a couple of days.

Today at the library he looked ashen and hangdog.

By way of explanation he said, "Tom came through." Hodge said he realized the last thing he needed was a drinking problem, so he'd asked him to leave. He said Tom got angry and hollered at him. But he was now gone, which was good. That was when he started avoiding the knock at the front door.

"But he told me a story," he said. "He said there was this guy in a wheelchair downtown whose charger for the chair had broken, so that he couldn't recharge his battery and move. He was just stranded in the middle of the sidewalk. So Tom paid someone five dollars for their shelter ticket, and gave it to the stranded wheelchair man, and somehow pushed the guy up toward the entrance of the shelter, but when the doorkeeper compared initials on the ticket to those in his notebook, they didn't match, and he wouldn't let the man in the wheelchair inside. A bit later, they discovered another man in a wheelchair who had the same battery charger, a functioning one, but when they asked if the first man could borrow it, the other man said no."

"And then what?"

He shrugged. "Then nothing. That's the end of the story."

TIDYMAN (BEN)

I took a short day on the railroad tracks today but picked the right spot. There's a shrine by the 82nd Avenue MAX stop, possibly at the very spot where the guy had crashed his car, and all the trash was making the shrine look bad. I did not go within ten feet of the shrine, mostly because I didn't trust myself not to take the full bottle of Heineken his friends had left there. After a few trains had gone past, I noticed a group of kids standing with their teacher on the MAX platform. I held the trash bag up and yelled, "I always got low marks in citizenship."

Most interesting find of the day: trophy from 1987 for Best Performance of "Walk Like an Egyptian." Not much else to report, except that there were a few tents at the overpass there, and as I was packing up, I spotted a man standing around. I took a funny cigarette from my pack, gave a peace sign, pointed at him and then at the cigarette. He strolled on over and we torched up. He told me he had some stuff if I knew anybody that was looking. I told him it wasn't my thing, but that I was sure someone was looking. "Yeah, but do they have any money?" he wanted to know. I left him with the big half of the cig and went on my way. Turns out he was leaving too, and he got up ahead of me and was greeted by a young lady at the crosswalk. I had lit up a cigarette, and the young lady, who had finished her conversation, asked me for one. I gave her a cig as we crossed the street. I needed time to finish mine before I went down the stairs to the platform, and I walked across the bridge to where I could get a good view to admire my work (looked much better). I rode back to the Rose Quarter and decided to walk to the Albina stop and maybe hit the big pile of trash across from the Coliseum, but there was a tent right next to it, and I was loath to get too close and disturb the occupants, and so moved on.

CATCHING STORIES (LAURA)

Outside the Hollywood Library, Hodge and I were scheming about how to finish our book once and for all, and what our next steps would look like if we did manage it. It was an unseasonably warm day in October, the sun shining and a mild breeze scattering the dry leaves at our feet. We drank coffee, mine with milk and Hodge's black.

"Are you doing okay?" I asked him. "I feel like I have less access to you."

He looked at me in surprise. "What? No, I'm fine. Well, I *was* going to say that I've gone irretrievably insane . . ."

"Yeah," I said. "Maybe that's what I'm picking up on."

"Maybe it's reading Alan Watts, you know, and wondering whether that has changed me in some way. Or reading Joseph Campbell. He says that we need a new mythology. The old ones are all dying."

"Hmm." I pinned a leaf with my foot and crunched it.

"You know," he continued. "It's the idea of how we don't come into this world. We come out of it."

I didn't really get it, but I told Hodge I did. Later, as I biked away and chewed on what he'd said, I felt it lifting off from the top of my head, felt those ideas flying away . . . I couldn't remember it anymore, not the parts I'd understood and surely not the parts I hadn't. How often had he given me some kind of brilliant if off-kilter story or philosophical musing that I'd failed to retain, even if I tried to write it down later? There were so many great moments that had evaporated in the face of my distraction. The best stories I'd ever heard had come from Hodge and from other patrons at the street library. And I felt despair because I would never be able to capture them all. I'd never be organized enough to put everything into a book.

I stopped my bike and propped it against a stop sign. I took off my helmet, hung it from the handlebars, and dialed him.

"I was thinking of what you said, about Watts and Campbell—will you tell me that again?"

"Oh yeah," he said. He didn't sound surprised to hear from me. "I'm glad you called because you know, you and me have these talks and then I keep thinking of things I never told you."

"That must be why I called." I rooted through my bag and pulled out an envelope to take notes on. "I'm ready."

TIDYMAN II (BEN)

If you're walking down the street and you see a little piece of scrap or a can or whatever, you can kick it, take a picture of it, blow on it, or whatever, and you will not have done anything wrong. But once you pick it up, it becomes your responsibility, and even if you put it back exactly where it was, you are guilty of littering. Technically, therefore, I am now guilty of several thousand separate counts of littering, and even John Grisham couldn't write me out of the mess I am in. I might spend the rest of my days behind bars for this.

Q: Is anyone paying you for this?

A: We are all paying for it every day, by having to look at it. The payments are getting smaller every week.

Q: Do you think that the people who are living out here have put it all here?

A: Some of it, probably, and I don't know what their shoe size is, but they got some of the smallest carbon footprints you can get.

Q: You're kind of a smartass, aren't you?

A: That'd be me.

HQ (LAURA)

The bulk of the administrative work for Street Books had always taken place on our respective kitchen tables, but I knew that somewhere in the city was a place for our organization to live, an office where we could settle in and trade our services for rent. I got a lot of faint smiles and pats during this time—given the real estate boom in Portland, it was hard to imagine we'd find a low-cost space for our headquarters.

An architect friend told me about the new affordable housing project she was working on and added, "I sure wish we could get Street Books in there." She put me in contact with a Person in Charge, whom I commenced emailing periodically over the next year. The complex would be located next to St. Francis, replacing the park and courtyard. By then, we had been holding library shifts for a few years outside the dining hall.

In the tradition of naming a place for what it previously contained (Quail Run, Hawk's View), the complex was called St. Francis Park Apartments. Eventually, miraculously, all the emailing paid off, and we were able to negotiate an agreement with the sponsoring agency, Catholic Charities, to take over a small room in exchange for operating an onsite library for the residents of the building. While the space may have been intended for storage—being mostly concrete with one wall of Sheetrock—it did have electricity, and once we filled it with a few desks, a couch, chairs, and two rugs (not to mention a thousand or so books), it was quite homey. It's hard to overstate what this meant to a small, scrappy street library, to have a place to store administrative stuff, library supplies, Armando, and a string of bike-shaped lights adorning one wall of bookshelves.

We moved in on a chilly afternoon in November 2017. The following month we held a cookie and cocoa party to spread the word about the new on-site library. Rain had typically closed down our operations on the book bike for a few months in winter, but suddenly we could stay open all year. Since a number of the folks at St. Francis were coming from lived experience on the streets, we would now be able to connect with library patrons indoors. Julie Keefe—who in 2012 had been named Portland's first Creative Laureate—set up a photo booth in one corner and people showed up in Christmas sweaters, wanting to have their portraits taken. It was not lost on me that we'd taken up residence a block from where I'd lived eighteen years earlier, at the corner of SE 12th and Oak. This was where I'd spoken with Quiet Joe about A. B. Guthrie Jr., and where Michael had come to my porch to give me my cut from the Harley Davidson gloves. It felt like coming home.

GALLANTRY (BEN)

Red Doors was closed again. We thought about trying Elephant Park or TPI, or maybe scouting around for a new
location. Then, since we hadn't been to Right to Dream since
they'd moved across the river, I suggested giving them a try
and left it up to Olive to decide. She'd joined the regular
Monday library shifts and was proving to be a valuable sidekick. She liked the Right to Dream option and we headed
for the bridge.

My leg had been giving me a good deal of trouble, so I
asked Olive if she wouldn't mind pushing the book bike up
the ramp while I went up the stairs. It was almost a washout
once we got there. Other than the gatekeeper and a few late
starters, the place was deserted. Back when they were still
at the Chinatown Gate, there were always a few regulars,
and of course a lot more foot traffic. Here, they did have the
advantage of storage shed–size dwellings, but I'm not sure
if that offsets what they lost by way of location. We picked
out fifteen or so books to stock their shelf and told them we
might see them down the road sometime.

Olive had been so gracious about pushing the bike up
the ramp that I volunteered to take it back down. I've always
prided myself on my gallantry. Then she got a phone call
and I found myself in Waterfront Park, well ahead of her.
Waiting there and sizing up the folks across the way and
thinking about opening up the book bike, I saw a guy raise

his arm and head my way, reaching into his pack. Obviously a book return. That was enough for me and I went over and set up the shelf, asking who wanted a book. Sure enough, they did, three of them, right about when Olive caught up. Then, as we ambled off, I spotted a Street Books sticker on a book in the hands of a person reading on a bench. The very same bench that I had sat on six years ago piling up my single-season record of fifty books. I wondered how long he was going to be out there.

LUCIDITY (LAURA)

I had a moment of lucidity on the corner of Sixth and Davis, outside Sisters of the Road. Diana and I set up the library, watching a man remove his shirt and sit in a straight-backed, lotus position. He was facing the sun, newly risen over Old Town, with his blond-gray hair feathered back seventies style, and a small stereo at his knee. Further down the sidewalk, someone was sleeping on a piece of cardboard. Nearby, several people sat at the curb and ran interference between two dogs that periodically barked and snarled at each other. Seventies Man was blasting songs and singing along.

His music became our soundtrack as we loaned books to patrons, moving from foot to foot, shimmying a little. On the bike library that day, we had a short story collection in Spanish by Junot Díaz, *Monster* by Walter Dean Myers, and Jane Smiley's *A Thousand Acres*. We had some Alice Walker and Tim O'Brien. A copy of *Death of a Salesman* by Arthur Miller marked with a note: HOLD FOR BARBIE.

There were so many stories behind the stories on the bike library. How Jane Smiley wrote *A Thousand Acres* as an allegory of *King Lear* to try and take tyranny down a peg. How Junot Díaz wrote his semi-autobiographical stories about his life as a Dominican immigrant and went on to publish a piece in the *New Yorker* about the abuse he'd suffered as a kid, and how he now faces allegations of harassing and abusing women and misusing his power as a gatekeeper. I surveyed the books and wondered if one should simply stay faithful to the stories inside the cover of each book, or was it necessary to also learn and know the stories that circle around the authors? In this crew was it enough to say that Walter Dean Myers wrote more than one hundred great books and never harassed anybody, or that Tim O'Brien brought a new literary quality to writing about the Vietnam War?

A girl in a long coat with faux fur edges tapped her cigarette and asked me if we had anything about the occult. She moved her hips to the music, taking puffs and blowing the smoke straight up. Alan didn't check out a book but instead told us that unfortunately he'd scored so high on an intelligence test that he is clinically insane. He pulled out two laminated four-leaf clovers from his wallet and told me to choose one. When I asked where he finds them, he told me about a place in Northwest, swearing me to secrecy. He leaned in close, "You don't just walk up to a four-leaf clover. You have to walk by with soft eyes, not be aggressive, and then it will reach out to you. It finds you first."

Meanwhile, the radio started to play Whitney Houston's version of "I Will Always Love You." We kept on checking out books, but now we were singing along while we filled out the library cards. When I looked up, I saw a kid walk by with an oversized rucksack on his back and a loping dog on a rope. He was lip-syncing to the chorus.

The music grew louder and I turned to find that Seventies Man had crossed the street to join us. He'd put on his shirt and a baseball cap and was carrying the little speaker under his arm. His pale white feet were bare, and he stood on his tiptoes, circling in a dance. Everyone danced now, and the words to the next song were familiar:

"Why do you build me up (build me up) buttercup baby just to let me down (let me down)." I recognized the song, but I didn't know until I looked it up later that it was record-ed by a band called The Foundations, a British soul band from the late sixties, composed of West Indians, White Brit-ish, and Sri Lankan musicians, a hodgepodge of different cultures and colors and ages and life experiences, a lot like the group of us out here.

We constituted our own interesting mix, a unique com-bo of dancers and nondancers, booklovers and nonreaders. There were those of us with plans, with tethers to the day in the form of a schedule or a place to be: kids coming home from school, a sofa with books piled on it, a cat looking for attention. And there were those whose plans consisted of re-turning to a spot near Skidmore Fountain or Forest Park or the waterfront, to a loading dock or an alley, whose priorities were to protect a backpack and bedroll; life goals winnowed down to simply staying alive, warm enough, fed enough. But for the length of a conversation about books on a street corner, these differences fell away.

For whatever reason, there were sparks inside that day. The magic came at that precise moment on that precise morning with its particular slant of granular late autumn light and the shadow that an oversized backpack casts. When I looked around slowly, I saw that it was like we were all on the set of a musical, inside the final scene where everything prior has built to this last song and dance, everyone spinning in their own orbit, yet in sync with one another: a garbage collec-tor with his trash-can dance moves; pedestrians stepping in unison, arms suddenly linked; and the shopkeeper emerging with her push broom, sweeping in time to the music.

LETTER TO JENNIFER

Dear Jennifer,

There's a risk of sounding like a sentimental fool here, but I still want to get it in the record.

We'll start with you. You look great, you're doing great, you are great, and seeing you again after all this time, and knowing that we'll be keeping in much closer touch, has left me with a feeling of peace and calm that I don't have words for, except those. Ineffable, I guess, is the word. It means: *cannot be put in to words.* I don't have the words to tell you how ineffable it is. And now we have so much to look forward to. I can see it all now. You'll be busy meeting the rest of the gang at the reunion, and I'll get shoved off to the side again, but that's okay, I'm used to that. This is going to be fun.

Franky is great. When you can manage to break through his cyberlife and find him, he's a blast. He dragged out the bat and balls and had me tossing him pitches for a while. Interesting that he knows about the sweet spot on the bat. He told me his dad showed him a few things about hitting. We had a pretty good snow fight too. I'm going to have to contrive some way to stay involved. Did I see something on your wall about him getting other kids interested in his books?

Tallulah I'm still trying to figure out. Is it because she's the younger one, or because she's a girl, or because she's the way she is, or is it all in my head? Whatever it is, she done got me. You probably didn't notice me doing it, but several times all I could do was just look at her, transfixed. And the way she took right to me, and picked up on my silly games and joined in. Both of them happy to have a whole extra bonus grand-dad and like that's what they expected all along. Obviously the groundwork you did has set the stage for making me feel so completely welcome. It's funny, all the other kids scream when I'm about to bite their toes, but Tula was perfectly content to let me eat all I wanted.

I had a clean shot at getting a look at that diary of hers when she left it behind on the window ledge and am proud to report that I did not peek, although I have heard rumors that the reason mothers give their teenage daughters diaries is so they can use their duplicate key to keep tabs on what their baby girls are up to.

Then there's seeing you all together. Them two getting along so well, rivalries notwithstanding, and you, caught in the never-ending struggle with the ever-changing limits, and the shifting sands of allegiance, and still being everybody's best pal. It's all just way too sweet, and I, for one, am never going to be the same. Not that I ever was the same, but you get the idea.

Mostly it was that everything felt so doggone right. Not just that they are fabulous kids, but that they are . . . mine. Almost like there must be some sort of a psychic connection that goes along with the blood tie, to the point where it borders on a physical thing that I can feel in my heart of hearts that wants to connect. And it is possible that that is only my imagination wanting it to be that way so that's how I feel it. But that's not what I think.

Ben

HEALTH REPORT (LAURA)

In Hergé's *Tintin and the Picaros*, Captain Haddock's whisky suddenly starts to taste wretched to him, even though it's usually his favorite drink. Every time he throws back a glass, he spits it out and hollers, "Blue blistering barnacles!" It turns out that the whole thing is an experiment by Professor Calculus to see whether he can cure Haddock of his booze habit.

I wish there were a pill I could drop in Hodge's drink that would help him quit the cigarettes. He tried the Wellbutrin but didn't like how it made him feel. There's a ticking clock here, though, since he's got thrombosis in both legs, some kind of circulatory problem that smoking makes worse. It will kill him if he doesn't get surgery, but the doc won't operate on Hodge if he's still smoking, because what's the point?

Sad things: thrombosis of the leg. Smoky lungs, hacking cough.

Heartening things: roof overhead, kitchen cupboards with food inside, carpet, a bed to sleep on, a writing desk. Hodge is doing well, even if his health is not great.

THE NICEST THING (BEN)

Street Books is a unique forum. We're a literacy project, a meeting place, an off-line chat room. It's certainly the only place I've ever seen four grown men standing around talking about how funny *I Love Lucy* was. Rachel and I were at TPI, and a guy was looking over the books while I was filing cards away, and I heard him say, "Whoa, that's the nicest thing anyone's ever said to me," and I said, "What did they say, I didn't hear." And he said, "She said, 'I like your socks.'" And I looked at him and said, "You don't get a ton of compliments, do you?" And he said, "What do you mean?" And I said, "Well . . . if the nicest thing anyone's ever said to you is 'I like your socks,' I don't know, maybe you should get out more? I don't mean . . . I'm sure you're out plenty, but, you know, broaden your horizons, meet new friends . . . no?"

Maybe you think that's a little unkind or insensitive, but flash back a few years to when that was me on the other side of the counter. Except don't stop there. Go back a few months before that, when, if I had seen the book bike, I would probably have done what we've all done before: looked away and kept walking, like it was some panhandler. Talking to people was not a happening deal back then. And those are the ones nobody ever sees.

The first-timers you spot right away, by their uncertainty. They look around, they ask, "So how does this work?" Sometimes I can't resist saying, "Not very well and not very often, but the idea is, you write your name on this card." Of course, the real idea is that you actually read the book. Or they ask, "So . . . when am I supposed to bring it back?" Lately I've taken to saying, "If you keep it longer than three weeks, you have to hand in a book report."

Then there was this guy just walking past. He'd only looked it over briefly when he said, "I'll tell you one thing. This is the nicest thing I've seen anyone do in this town." And went on his way.

OLD CROW (LAURA)

I sat in Hodge's smoky apartment while he paced around, and I watched the bandage on his foot slowly come loose as he tracked it behind him. He looked like an unraveling mummy. Diana came by and both of us entreated him to sit on the futon and elevate his leg, but he was sauced and stubborn and said we were stupid to be fussing at him so. How sauced he was, we couldn't know exactly. But he cracked a second Hamm's in the middle of the afternoon and mentioned taking the Vicodin in the night when he'd had terrible pain. The short version of the story is that the doctor had finally decided to operate and Hodge'd had a bypass surgery on his leg a week ago, leaving him with a crazy incision from his inner thigh next to his groin down to below his knee on the right leg. Decided to go home from the VA hospital instead of going to a rehabilitation center for a few days. Both the vascular surgeon and the nurse gave him the go-ahead if that was his choice, so it was hard to argue against them. But what it meant was that he was at home tracking his bandage around, drunk.

Last night (what set off the whole thing in the first place), he decided to walk to New Seasons for beer and bagels, and by the time he returned, he realized he'd overdone it, and in the middle of the night he'd had terrible burning in both feet and I got a text that referred to an adventure he'd had and how maybe it would change our plans for the next day (which were loose anyway). Now he just kept saying, "What are we gonna do? Let's go ahead with our plan," and I felt so frustrated with him and his stubbornness. And so scared that he'd had a major surgery and then was back home smoking cigarettes end to end and drinking beer and taking Vicodin and staggering around the house. Mad that he didn't take better care of himself and scared that I'd someday come to his house and find him dead.

I told him that I understood that he might not have a lot of say over the intense pull of the cig-and-Hamm sandwich, so from this point onwards I was going to try and avoid being mad at him about it. Instead, I was going to visualize a sooty old crow, about Hodge's height, whose wings give off puffs of soot whenever he moves around. That's who I'd be mad at for these vices, that fucking Sooty Crow.

There is every kind of way to look at it. Hodge used to sleep on Davis Street outside of the boarded-up Chinese restaurant. He slept on the sidewalk, wearing the same pair of pants he'd had on for six months. He had an apartment now, a kitchen and bathroom and bedroom, a postal address. Those were good things and worth holding up against the unraveling bandage. I'd seen bandaged men with hospital bracelets still on their wrists heading back to their campsites. Things could always be worse.

OUTREACH (BEN)

There's a church up behind the library that serves a lunch on Mondays and Thursdays, and I still go there on Mondays once in a while, since I'm already in town after the shift. Now you might wonder why I would wait in line for an hour for a meal that's on par with Mission food. Actually it's one of the better meals in town. I don't eat that good at home sometimes. And once in a while I'll see someone reading a book that they got from the book bike earlier that same day. I don't always talk to them, but a few weeks back I was telling a guy that I was back indoors now, mostly by being lucky, and he told me that he was fairly new to being outdoors and didn't know what he was going to do. I told him it's a long way from here to there and that's about the best I can tell you.

FULL CIRCLE (LAURA)

Celia, who had been Street Books' very first volunteer back when she was my student at Lincoln High School, dropped in at HQ to visit with me and Hodge. She now worked for Outside In, an organization that has provided health care and other services to underserved people in Portland since the late sixties. We talked about how perfect it was that all these years later she would go into social services herself. She went on to tell us about her one and only Tinder date, which she'd agreed to go on only to prove to her friends that it's a terrible platform and wouldn't work for her. She'd invited her date to watch *Sorry to Bother You*, and knew even before the film, when they were still having a drink, that it would never work. But she went anyway. I shook my head and clucked sympathetically, giving unsolicited advice here and there. Hodge said, "Maybe what's going on is that dating, as you know it, is simply one of the most inefficient, nonproductive, haphazard, and hit-or-miss ways to try and achieve one of the most important objectives of your life. It's time to do something different." We looked at him with surprise and then saw that he was reading from the back of a Dr. Phil book called *Love Smart*.

HAPPINESS (BEN)

It has to come from inside. You cannot give someone a happiness transplant, and back when I was feeling really bad, I even said it back then: somebody could give me $50,000 and it wouldn't help. It wouldn't have amounted to much more than 50,000 problems that I couldn't handle. You get a severely depressed person, and about the best you can do is hope they don't go through with it.

VARIOUS KINDS OF ENDINGS (LAURA)

It wasn't so difficult to stake a flag at the beginning. This was clear enough to both of us: Skidmore Fountain; Portland, Oregon. June 2011. The man who I would come to know as Ben Hodgson wore a scuffed-up jacket and hair that curled over his collar, a feral beard, "the unwashed phenomenon, the original vagabond," as Joan Baez used to sing. We stood and looked at the bike library together and talked about Wodehouse and indeed, this became one of our best stories: the one in which Hodge meets this woman standing with a rolling bicycle contraption full of books and asks, "And where, pray tell, is the Wodehouse?" And said woman, who Hodge will come to know as Laura Moulton, gets nervous, as in "I've heard of Wodehouse but never met him . . ." to which Hodge responds, "What kind of librarian doesn't keep Wodehouse on the shelf?"

Easy enough to pinpoint the start. It's the ending that presents a challenge. A moving target. Hodge will tell a funny or touching story about his library shift in Old Town and I'll laugh or whistle, "Wow, that's a good one," and he'll say, "Maybe that's it right there—we end our book right there." But the next day there is more to the story.

VOICEMAIL FOR LAURA

"I'm leaning toward an 'in medias res' deal that is immediately introspective: describing a state of mind that is approaching breakdown stage, how trapped I felt, how I saw it coming and was still too helpless to do anything to prepare for it, and how quickly I sank into the whirlpool. Something like: 'Knowing what I know now, I can almost see why I was so helpless and freaked while my whole life crashed.' Then, a quick description of the pitch, and how my efforts were destined to come up short. Then Old Town, and make it creepy. Get a real good feel of the bleakness, then the quick alleviation with the first winter indoors after all. And even that was still alienating as hell, and back on the sidewalk five months later and no better off."

NITE HAWK

JANUARY 2, 2019—RECORDING OF A CONVERSATION AT NITE HAWK CAFÉ & LOUNGE

L: You were saying something about special circumstances posing challenges to our book?

B: Yeah, well Jennifer and the kids came into my life—it just changed everything. And I don't really care about anything else right now.

L: Oh great.

B: Who cares about writing a dopey book, you know?

L: Well, I'm glad to know that. But you might have a stray day here or there that you could—

B: I called them up at exactly 8:59 p.m. our time, New Year's Eve, and I was just going to say, "Okay, I gotta go, I'll talk to you next year," and then hang up and call them right back and say, "See I told you I'd talk to you next year—how you been doing since I talked to you last?" But it turns out they were away at a party. Anyway, I been thinking about writing other things and emailing those to you.

L: I think you should. That thing I sent you about lucidity? About the shift at Sixth and Davis? Remember that? The guy has the stereo and everybody's dancing and it turns into this sensation of a musical? Anyway, I think side-writing is great. Like stepping out on your main project and doing a little something, like you're meeting illicitly with another project?

B: Is that running? *(points at recorder)*

A FEW WORDS ABOUT LAURA

AS TOLD TO THE GERMAN DOCUMENTARY CREW

"You've only known Laura for five days and *you* love her. So that's a few words about Laura. She's irresistible. She just got a bright idea one day and said, 'I think I'll go ride my bike around and see if people want to read these books.' People did want to read the books. That was eight years ago."

BE HERE NOW (LAURA)

It was a sweet day at the corner of SE 12th and Ash, and Hodge and I were sitting in the sun outside of Triumph Coffee. A woman approached and sat at the next table over. She had a beautiful dog, a kind of husky maybe, one eye white-blue, the other one brown. He was gray around his muzzle and ears, and he gave my hand a polite sniff before he settled down at my feet.

We'd been talking about mortality. Hodge's brother-in-law, Blaine, had just lost a son, age forty, who'd apparently had a heart problem. Hodge couldn't get over how devastating this must be, losing a child, no matter what age. His kids are both adults now and his daughter has kids of her own. He has been at times unmoored by how much he loves those kids. Mine are still growing out of childhood and the idea of losing them punched me in the solar plexus.

The woman stood and tugged at the leash. "Roscoe, c'mon, we're going to the dog store for treats." But Roscoe wasn't having any of it. He'd only just settled down in the shade of the picnic table alongside the café and he wanted to stay there. Hodge laughed his raspy cough-laugh. He has a deep appreciation for anyone who doesn't follow the rules, including dogs.

"That's a rugged cough, Hodge," I said. "Maybe you should read that book Johannes gave you." Johannes was the videographer on the German film crew who'd shot the documentary about Street Books. He'd given a book to Hodge as a parting gift. He said it had helped him quit smoking after years of not being able to kick it.

Hodge shrugged. "Yes, perhaps I should." But he didn't sound convinced.

"How about this," I said. "How about you read that book carefully for ten minutes each day to investigate how it won't help you? To explore the ways it will fail?"

He grinned at this—he could see right through me.

"You cannot rip the skin off the snake," he said. "The snake sheds its skin at the rate it does—that's just the way it happens."

"Wow, that's heavy, Hodge."

"It's Ram Dass," he said. "*Be Here Now*."

THE STREET BOOKS SPECIAL (BEN)

"Hey, Street Books here. Got books. Get your books. Got *Nineteenth Century Russia*. Got *Miss Pickerell Goes to Mars*. Don't miss the July special."

"What special?"

"For the whole month, you get a book, you want to read it twice, that's perfectly okay with us, no extra charge."

"You don't charge anything anyway, and I could read it twice even if it wasn't okay with you."

"There's no deceiving you, sir. You are so very right; you surely could do just exactly that. But, you could not do it at the same time we were running the special."

He took two copies of *Nineteenth Century Russia*.

HOW TO RUN A
STREET LIBRARY

1. **Overview:** Be aware of where your patrons will be and of who they are. Pay attention to where in your city houseless people congregate, where meals are available, where camps are established, and who's already out there working in the community.

2. **Books:** Stock your library. Gather donations from housed folks, discards from public libraries, gently used titles from your local independent bookstore. This is the easy part—people love to donate books!
    a. You can start a street library with as few as twenty books. (Don't worry, your collection will grow.) The books should be good, with something for every taste. It's important to provide a diversity of titles—books by and about people of color, trans folks, books in a variety of languages—so that patrons see themselves reflected in the selection.
    b. Emphasize paperbacks! Hardcover books are difficult to carry.
    c. As you get to know your individual patrons, ask them what they're interested in reading, and seek out those titles and genres. Curation for each specific shift is a good idea.

3. **Location:** Choose a regular spot. Set up at the same time and place each week so that patrons can rely on your service, return books, and check out new ones. (At Street Books

we set up shifts at a respectful distance from where people might gather for a meal or other services. This way we get a concentration of folks all together and they can choose to come to us.)

    a. Be patient—it takes time to establish trust.

    b. It's so important to offer a welcoming greeting. Learn and remember names. Engage with the patrons and get to know them on their terms.

    c. People will gradually get comfortable with you and realize that the books are free and that the project is expressly for them. Be friendly and approachable but try not to overwhelm your patrons.

4. **Library Infrastructure:**

    a. Bicycles are the best, for mobility and weight. Something as small as a bike basket will work, but the best-case scenario is if you're able to carry between forty and fifty books and also display them in a way that allows passersby to peruse titles without having to commit completely.

    b. Our informal "script" when people approach: "Hey there, we've got books here for you. We're a street library, so there are no fees or fines. Check out a book and return it next week. Or if we don't cross paths, pass it on to someone who would like to read it."

    c. It's also great to offer reading glasses, in a variety of strengths—so many people need them.

5. **Security:** At Street Books we have a policy that if anyone ever feels unsafe at the shift, they should simply close up and ride the bike away. In an emergency, it's fine to just leave the bike and make a hasty exit. (That said, we've never

had an incident where librarians felt truly in peril. In fact, the opposite is generally true: With the loyalty we've built up with our patrons, we actually feel safer because so many folks now have our back.)

6. **Systems:** Keep it simple.
   a. Use a clipboard for recording the number of books and reading glasses dispensed, and a narrative of the shift. (You'll want to jot down the weather, the anecdotes, the requests.)
   b. A log can be helpful for tracking the most popular titles, and it can also help you provide data to foundations or individual donors who might want to know your circulation numbers.

7. **Sustainability:** You can start a street library all by yourself (Laura did). But soon you will likely want partners, more librarians, and supporters. You might need to raise money, collect materials, and consider becoming a nonprofit organization in order to keep the library going.

8. **It's Fun:** That's the purpose, really. Humor and connection.

9. **Things to Remember:**
   a. Don't assume anything about anyone.
   b. Biggest contributors to being outside in the first place: wealth inequality and structural racism. It's important to know what's going on in your city (i.e., sit-lie ordinances, sweeps, anticamping policies, etc.).
   c. Street Books is not a charity or social service agency, but more of a collaboration. We seek to engage in

dialogue and create interaction around books. We are grateful that people who are living with this level of deprivation and stress are still keen to make time to come see us and to read books.

d. Respect your patrons and their desire to read. We once had a guy turn down Nietzsche, not because he didn't want to read Nietzsche, but because it was the wrong translation.

e. Maintain a loose return policy. Prioritize books circulating on the streets over books coming back to you (and remember that it's very hard to keep books in good condition in the outdoors).

f. In our experience, the majority of people living outside are glad to see us and want to read books. But it's also true that they're dealing with a level of trauma or sadness that we don't understand, and at times it may be that a paperback book is not what they most need.

Whenever you have questions or are feeling uncertain or discouraged, feel free to contact Street Books to talk with an experienced librarian. We may not have the answers, but we'd love to help you think through the challenges.

librarian@streetbooks.org

ACKNOWLEDGMENTS (LAURA)

Hodge and I have joked about writing a sequel that is five hundred pages long, full of all the stories that didn't make it into this book. It would take a volume that size just to capture the gratitude I feel toward the people who have been instrumental in the making of this book, and in the creation of the Street Books project.

The Book:

Thank you, Hodge, for busting my chops about not having P. G. Wodehouse in the library but coming back the next week anyway. Thanks to Michael Heald, who knew exactly what to do with the pages we gave him. To ace editor Alissa Hattman, for helping us recognize we were further along than we thought. To Aaron Miller, who took his sketch-book to the places we described and captured the essence of our story with his beautiful art. To Esa Grigsby, for the limerick, and for leaving an incisive and generous mark on this book. To my writing community who offered encour-agement, listened to early drafts, and checked in on how the project was coming along: Martha Gies, Lisa Hoashi, Re-becca Koffman, Patricia Kullberg, Joanne Mulcahey, Kim Stafford, Judith Arcana, and David Naimon. To the One Page Wednesday crew for literary fellowship and delicious dinners: Natalie Serber, Mary Rechner, Sarah Sentilles,

Robin Romm, Emily Chenoweth, Sue Hill, and Peyton Marshall. To Ben Waterhouse and *Oregon Humanities* for bringing Hodge's story to more readers. To Joanne Zuhl and *Street Roots* for publishing some of the first pages of this book. To my colleagues at Literary Arts and the high school students I've had the pleasure of working with for the past twenty years.

For ongoing support of the Street Books project and a willingness to put their names on this book: Karen Russell, Peter Rock, Rene Denfeld, and Omar El Akkad.

To Jodi Darby and Marisa Anderson for friendship and for granting me the El Rancho writing residency where a number of these pages were written. To Caroline Oakley and Wendy Marich for co-parenting my kids and helping to create the space for me to write.

The Library:

Thank you to our library patrons. Thank you Diana Rempe for building this project with me, for the years of friendship, and for talking me off innumerable cliffs. Thank you to the Street Books team, past and present: Celia Luce, Sue Zalokar, Ben Hodgson, Beth Chapman, Redd Moon, Diana Rempe, Tracy Rimel, Austin Allstadt, Robin Schauffler, Ben Parzybok (for all things tech), Amy Dennis, Amy Bradley, Maria Power, Sharon Gregory, Betsy & Jim Holzgraf, Byrd, Rachel Dawson, Pépe Espinoza, Olive Alsept Ellis, Merüch, Pati Moran, Marissa Santillán-Guzmán, River Enza, Lori Woolf-Pollock, Nika Clark, Lucie Bonvalet, Katy Stevens, John Boelling, Sofie Jokela, Monica Beemer, Security Steve,

Rob at Monte Rossa Café (for the hospitality & restroom), and Trent DeBord. To Julie Keefe, our stellar House Photographer. To Patrick Crowley, who launched our first sister street library, Street Books ATX.

For support and vital counsel over the years, thank you to Israel Bayer, Dick Adams, Robyn Steely, Kaia Sand, Kathy Kniep, George Thorn, and Alison Bailey.

To the generous independent bookstores and publishers who have supported us: Microcosm Publishing, Annie Bloom's, Broadway Books, Powell's Books, Tom Murray & Artifacts, Second Glance Books, Rhonda Hughes & Hawthorne Books, and Tavern Books.

To Geoff Brunk and the Multnomah County Library for all the postal courtesy returns!

To Kirk Johnson of the *New York Times* for capturing the Street Books magic in print, and to Michael Bernstein, Marina Samokhina, and Johannes Straub at Bernsteinfilm for the lovely documentary. To Anne Rosellini and Debra Granik for including us in the research process of their film, *Leave No Trace*.

For their generous support: Craig Haynes and the City of Portland, the Meyer Foundation, the National Book Foundation, Regional Arts & Culture Council, New Seasons, the Millsdavis Foundation, the Awesome Foundation, the Collins Foundation, SE Uplift, Humble Bundle, Oregon Community Foundation, Oregon Cultural Trust, Multnomah County Cultural Coalition, the OCF Joseph E. Weston

Public Foundation, and Andy McMillan and Andy Baio with XOXO. To Margot Atwell from Kickstarter.

Thanks to former City Commissioner Amanda Fritz, who always made time to speak at our events, and to former Commissioner Chloe Eudaly, Commissioner Jo Ann Hardesty, and County Commissioner Sharon Meieran for their support.

To my parents, Roy and Dottie Moulton, who have never missed a Street Books event (and thanks for doing the desserts, Ma!). To James, who built the bike library and took it for the first test ride. To Coen and Sylvie, who have grown up stepping over endless stacks of books—may you always be surrounded by this kind of wealth.

Finally, to Ben Parzybok, my literary compatriot, my sidekick and co-conspirator. Thank you for listening to my first ideas and helping to make them better. Thank you for the grand adventures we've had and for everything to come.

ACKNOWLEDGMENTS (BEN)

Jennifer Lee, Franklin Andrew, and Tallulah Isabel Revy. You are the light of my life, my favorite people in the whole world, and who needs dumb old books when I have you guys?

John Colvin, the only person in two whole years who showed me anything I could put to use. That you could go to Waterfront Park and sleep, that the Hawthorne Bridge worked for a rain shelter. And that, when told to leave any particular spot, you simply left and waited for the authorities to leave, then went back. It was grief enough just being outside, and any tools one has make a big difference. Thank you, John.

Hayseed, who actually was in Vietnam, and is the true source of the idea for the STILL CRAZY AFTER THAT ONE YEAR sign.

Jarvis Allen, case manager extraordinaire, without whose efforts I could be living in a big pile of garbage somewhere for all I know, trying to dig my way out, like some mole that was in a big pile of garbage.

Laura Moulton, of course, who came up with the clever idea of writing a book, and took my scribblings and rearranged them into something coherent. Laura is the best.

Alissa Hattman, who took two folders full of disorganized ramblings and assembled them into a more or less sensible arrangement.

And don't let us forget Michael Heald, who saw that it could be done, and coaxed us into actually doing it, after interminable delays of our own making. Amazing work, Michael.

And thanks Josh, for being a pal these past seven years.

And most of all, Armando, who never complained once in spite of intolerable indignities for which I am truly abashed, ashamed, repentant, and looking for the chance to do it all again.